Essential Life Skills for Every 13-Year-Old

A Teen's Guide to Unlocking Hidden Strengths for Achievement, Wellness, and Joy

Mark Lee

Mark Lee © Copyright 2025. All rights reserved.

The content contained within this book may not be reproduced, duplicated, or transmitted without direct written permission from the author or the publisher. Under no circumstances will any blame or legal responsibility be held against the publisher, or author, for any damages, reparation, or monetary loss due to the information contained within this book, either directly or indirectly.

Legal Notice:
This book is copyright-protected. It is only for personal use. You cannot amend, distribute, sell, use, quote or paraphrase any part, or the content within this book, without the consent of the author or publisher.

Disclaimer Notice:
Please note the information contained within this document is for educational and entertainment purposes only. All effort has been executed to present accurate, up-to-date, reliable, and complete information. No warranties of any kind are declared or implied. Readers acknowledge that the author is not engaging in the rendering of legal, financial, medical or professional advice. The content within this book has been derived from various sources. Please consult a licensed professional before attempting any techniques outlined in this book.
By reading this document, the reader agrees that under no circumstances is the author responsible for any losses, direct or indirect, that are incurred as a result of the use of the information contained within this document, including, but not limited to, errors, omissions, or inaccuracies

Table of Contents

Chapter 1: Introduction to Life Skills 5
    The Power of Mastering Life Skills 6
    How to Use This Book Effectively 9

Chapter 2: Understanding and Managing Emotions 11
    Emotional Intelligence and Its Importance 12
    Identifying and Expressing Your Feelings 14

Chapter 3: Building Confidence and Self-Esteem 17
    Positive Self-Talk for Confidence and Empowerment 18
    Overcoming Self-Doubt in Everyday Life 19

Chapter 5: Smart Goal Setting 21
    Setting Realistic and Achievable Goals 22
    Tracking Progress and Celebrating Milestones 24

Chapter 6: Study Skills and Learning Strategies 27
    Effective Note-Taking Strategies 29
    Test Preparation Tips and Study Strategies 31

Chapter 7: Communication Skills for Everyday Life 35
    Active Listening and Clear Communication Skills 36
    Understanding Nonverbal Communication 37

Chapter 8: Healthy Relationships and Friendships 39
    Building Trust and Positive Friendships 41
    Setting Boundaries and Assertive Communication 42

Chapter 10: Making Good Decisions 45
    Making Thoughtful Decisions Every Day 46
    Learning from Mistakes for Better Decisions 48

Chapter 11: Digital Citizenship and Online Safety 49
    Protecting Your Privacy and Digital Reputation 51
    Kind, Responsible, and Respectful Online 53

Chapter 12: Financial Literacy for Beginners 57
    Money Basics and Smart Budgeting 59
    Smart Choices: Saving, Spending, and Financial Goals 61

Chapter 1: Introduction to Life Skills

Have you ever considered the practical implications of having superpowers? Imagine confidently navigating complex situations, making strategic decisions that lead to real success, and building strong, lasting relationships. While you may not have the ability to fly or become invisible, you possess essential skills that can help you achieve these outcomes and more. Known as life skills, these abilities are crucial for unlocking your potential and evolving into the best version of yourself.

Life skills are like the essential tools in a superhero's utility belt. They empower you to face challenges, devise solutions, and seize opportunities. Whether you're tackling a tough homework assignment, resolving a conflict with a peer, or improving your time management strategies, these skills provide the framework for effective decision-making. They are vital for personal development and success, not just in academic settings but in all areas of life.

This book serves as your comprehensive guide to identifying and refining these skills. Throughout its chapters, you will explore topics such as emotional intelligence, time management, financial literacy, and more. Each chapter is thoughtfully crafted to provide both theoretical knowledge and practical exercises that help you apply what you've learned in real-world contexts. Reflection sections prompt you to analyze your experiences and consider how to use your newly acquired abilities for improvement.

In today's world, life skills are more important than ever. They enhance your ability to communicate effectively, foster healthy relationships, and navigate the complexities of the digital environment with confidence. Whether you're engaging with classmates, forming new friendships, or participating in online discussions, these skills enable you to make informed choices and stand out as a leader.

As you journey through this book, you'll notice a structured approach that makes learning enjoyable and effective. Each chapter focuses on a specific skill, breaking it down into manageable components with clear explanations and relevant examples. You'll find "Try This" activity boxes that encourage you to apply your skills in practical scenarios, along with summaries that reinforce your understanding. By the end of each chapter, you'll have a deeper grasp of the skill and its potential benefits.

Keep in mind that developing life skills is an ongoing process rather than a finite goal. This journey involves continuous growth, learning, and increasing independence. As you engage in this process, remember the insight from

Albert Einstein: "The only source of knowledge is experience." Embrace the experiences that come your way and use them as opportunities for learning and personal development.

The Power of Mastering Life Skills

Starting your journey to master life skills can feel overwhelming, but remember: you don't have to do it all at once! Pick one skill—like time management or emotional intelligence—and focus on small, daily improvements. Celebrate your progress, no matter how minor it seems. Over time, these small steps add up, helping you become more confident, independent, and ready to handle whatever life throws your way.

Mastering life skills provides a comprehensive toolkit that helps you tackle everyday challenges with confidence. Imagine attending a social gathering and feeling completely at ease while engaging with others, or managing your schedule so effectively that you excel academically while still making time for your favorite activities. These examples show how such skills can significantly enhance daily interactions and improve your overall quality of life.

Emotional intelligence stands out as one of the most important life skills. It involves recognizing, understanding, and managing emotions in a positive way. This skill acts as a sophisticated system for evaluating emotional states, helping you navigate the complex world of feelings. You gain insight into your emotional responses and those of your peers. For instance, if you feel anxious before an important exam, this awareness allows you to recognize that feeling and apply strategies to ease it, such as practicing deep breathing or using positive visualization techniques. If a friend seems upset, your ability to empathize and offer support can really strengthen your relationships.

Time management is another essential skill for balancing academic responsibilities, personal interests, and social activities. Picture your day as a structured framework, with each segment dedicated to a specific task. Effective time management enables you to combine all these elements smoothly, reducing feelings of being overwhelmed. Prioritizing tasks and setting realistic goals helps you allocate enough time for studying, participating in sports, socializing with friends, and enjoying leisure activities. For example, creating a daily planner or using digital scheduling tools can help you keep track of assignments and deadlines, reducing stress and boosting your overall productivity.

Financial literacy may seem more relevant to adults, but it is equally important for teenagers. Understanding the basics of budgeting and saving can set the stage for future financial stability. Think about receiving your allowance or earning money from a part-time job. Instead of spending all your funds right away, this knowledge teaches you to divide your earnings into categories:

some for savings, some for discretionary spending, and possibly some for charitable contributions. This method encourages thoughtful financial decision-making, ensuring you have resources for the things and experiences that truly matter.

Real-life examples of teenagers successfully managing these skills can be incredibly inspiring. Take, for instance, a 14-year-old who started a small business selling handmade crafts. She effectively balanced academic responsibilities with her entrepreneurial efforts by using time management techniques. Her emotional intelligence helped her respond positively to customer feedback, while financial literacy enabled her to budget her profits wisely, reinvesting in her business while saving for future goals.

As you develop these life skills, you will likely notice a shift in your mindset. This is where the idea of a growth mindset comes into play. A growth mindset is the belief that you can improve your abilities and intelligence through dedication and effort. It involves welcoming challenges, learning from mistakes, and persisting in the face of difficulties. When you approach situations with this mindset, you view challenges as opportunities for learning and growth rather than obstacles to avoid. This perspective not only boosts your confidence but also nurtures resilience and adaptability.

A growth mindset is a powerful concept that can significantly impact personal development. It's the belief that abilities and intelligence can be developed through dedication, effort, and structured learning. This mindset encourages viewing challenges as opportunities for growth rather than barriers to success. Embracing this perspective makes you more inclined to take calculated risks and explore new avenues, knowing that even if you stumble, you'll gain valuable insights and experience along the way. This approach fosters resilience, a crucial trait that helps you bounce back from setbacks and persist in your efforts.

Facing challenges and learning from failures are key components of developing resilience. When you encounter a difficult situation, choosing to confront it directly is empowering. This doesn't mean you'll be free from feelings of anxiety or uncertainty; rather, it shows a willingness to navigate those emotions to uncover your potential. Each time you successfully overcome a challenge, your confidence in managing future difficulties grows. When mistakes happen, viewing them as essential learning experiences instead of failures is incredibly beneficial. This shift in perspective allows for critical analysis of what went wrong, making necessary adjustments, and approaching the situation again with a refined strategy.

Goal setting serves as another essential tool for achieving personal aims and overcoming obstacles. Establishing clear, achievable goals creates a structured plan for progress. One effective method for setting goals involves the SMART criteria, which stands for Specific, Measurable, Achievable, Relevant, and Time-bound. Let's break this down:

1. **Specific**: Clearly define the goal so you know exactly what you're aiming for. Instead of saying, "I want to do better in school," specify, "I want to raise my math grade from a B to an A."

2. **Measurable**: You need a quantifiable way to track progress. This could involve monitoring grades, test scores, or receiving feedback from teachers.

3. **Achievable**: The goal should be realistic and attainable. It's important to set a goal that challenges you while remaining within your capabilities.

4. **Relevant**: The goal should align with broader objectives and hold significance. If improving your math grade is crucial for your future academic plans, it is relevant.

5. **Time-bound**: Establish a deadline for the goal. This helps maintain focus and motivation. For example, you might aim to achieve it by the end of the semester.

To practice setting SMART goals, try this exercise: Identify an area in your life where you want to improve. Write down a specific goal using the SMART criteria. Then, outline the steps needed to achieve it. This could include dedicating a specific number of hours each day to studying, seeking assistance from a teacher, or utilizing online resources for additional practice.

Self-reflection plays a critical role in personal development. It involves taking time to analyze experiences, actions, and outcomes. Reflecting on past actions helps pinpoint areas of excellence and those needing improvement. This process enhances your understanding of strengths and weaknesses, enabling informed decisions about future actions. For instance, if you recognize struggles with time management, you can focus on developing strategies to better organize your schedule.

Cultivating a growth mindset, confronting challenges, and setting SMART goals shows that these skills apply not only to personal development but also to academic success. The ability to view challenges as opportunities, learn from mistakes, and establish clear goals will serve you well in an educational environment. Whether tackling a difficult subject, preparing for exams, or collaborating on a group project, these skills will help you navigate the demands of school life with confidence and resilience.

To achieve academic success, cultivating effective study techniques and organizational skills is essential. Establishing a dedicated study space that minimizes distractions is a practical strategy. This area should be well-lit, ergonomically designed for comfort, and stocked with necessary materials, including specific notebooks for different subjects, high-quality pens, and a reliable computer with access to educational resources. Maintaining a consistent environment signals to your brain that it's time to focus, enhancing concentration and productivity.

How to Use This Book Effectively

To unlock your unique capabilities, it's important to first understand the structure of this book. Think of it as a detailed framework that guides you through specific life skills essential for achieving success, maintaining health, and cultivating happiness. Start with the table of contents, which serves as a comprehensive guide to the topics covered. Each chapter focuses on a particular skill, such as emotional intelligence or time management, and includes subheadings that make navigation a breeze.

Once you grasp the overall structure, dive into the chapters that spark your interest. Whether you aim to enhance your communication skills or gain insights into financial literacy, the table of contents will help you find relevant information quickly. While reading, pay close attention to the "Try This" activity boxes. These sections provide practical exercises and real-world applications of the skills discussed, allowing you to practice and internalize the concepts. Engaging with these activities will deepen your understanding and make the learning experience more interactive and enjoyable.

At the end of each chapter, you will find reflective questions that encourage critical analysis of the material. These prompts aim to foster self-reflection and enhance self-awareness. Take time to engage with them, as they will enrich your comprehension and help you apply the skills in your everyday life. The bullet points summarizing key concepts also serve as handy reference tools, encapsulating the main ideas for easy review and reinforcement of your learning.

Visual learners will appreciate the images included throughout the book. These visuals are thoughtfully chosen to enhance memory retention and clarify the concepts presented. Use them as aids to help recall information and solidify your understanding of the material.

Consider creating a personal plan or journal to track your progress as you develop these skills. Inspired by the actionable tips provided, document your goals, reflections, and insights gained throughout the process. This practice will keep you organized and motivated, allowing you to monitor advancements and identify areas that need further attention.

Remember that learning is a continuous journey. Revisit chapters periodically to reinforce your understanding and integrate new insights as you grow. As you continue to develop these life skills, they will become instinctive, equipping you to navigate the complexities of adolescence and beyond with confidence and resilience.

Chapter 2: Understanding and Managing Emotions

Emotional intelligence serves as a powerful tool that can greatly influence personal growth and relationships. At its core, it involves understanding and managing your own emotions while being attuned to the feelings of others. This skill is essential for navigating the complexities of adolescence and beyond, as it helps you make informed decisions, build strong connections, and handle challenges with grace.

Let's define some key terms. **Emotions** are complex reactions that encompass both cognitive processes and physiological responses. Specific events, thoughts, or interpersonal interactions can trigger them, and they often influence behavior and decision-making. **Emotional awareness** refers to recognizing and understanding your emotions as they arise, forming the foundation for effectively managing feelings. **Emotional regulation** involves controlling emotional responses to ensure they are appropriate for the context. This approach does not mean suppressing emotions but rather managing them constructively to promote positive outcomes.

Emotions significantly impact daily life and decision-making. For example, experiencing happiness can boost motivation and creativity, while sadness may lead to increased reflection and caution. Anger can drive you to confront injustices, but if not managed properly, it can escalate into conflict. Fear acts as a protective mechanism against danger, yet excessive fear might prevent you from pursuing new opportunities. Recognizing these emotions and their physical manifestations—such as a racing heart when anxious or a warm sensation when happy—enables more effective responses.

To accurately identify and label your emotions, try this exercise: Throughout the day, pause and ask yourself, "What am I feeling right now?" Document your emotions in a journal, noting any accompanying physical sensations or thoughts. Over time, this practice will enhance emotional awareness and help you identify patterns in your responses.

You can develop the skill of managing emotions through consistent practice. One effective strategy involves mindfulness, which focuses your attention on the present moment without judgment. Concentrating on your breath or the physical sensations in your body creates a space between emotions and reactions, allowing you to choose a more deliberate response. Deep breathing serves as another powerful technique. When feeling overwhelmed, take slow, deep breaths to calm your nervous system and regain a sense of control. Positive self-talk also proves beneficial; replace negative thoughts with affirmations such as "I can handle this" or "I am capable."

Empathy, the ability to understand and share the feelings of others, constitutes a crucial component of emotional intelligence. Considering someone else's perspective allows you to appreciate their feelings better and respond with compassion. This understanding can strengthen relationships and facilitate more effective conflict resolution. For instance, if a friend is upset, acknowledging their feelings and offering support can significantly impact their ability to cope with the situation.

Imagine a scenario where effective emotion management leads to a positive outcome. Picture yourself in a disagreement with a friend. Instead of reacting with anger, take a moment to breathe deeply and reflect on their perspective. Calmly expressing your feelings and actively listening to theirs can help you reach a resolution that satisfies both parties, thereby strengthening your friendship in the process.

To track your progress in managing emotions, maintain a journal where you record your responses and the strategies you employed to address them. Reflect on what worked well and what could be improved. This practice will help you build emotional resilience, the capacity to recover from setbacks and adapt to change.

Developing emotional intelligence is an ongoing process that requires time and effort. Be patient with yourself and acknowledge your progress along the way. Here are some actionable tips for building resilience: practice gratitude by noting specific things you're thankful for each day, engage in regular physical activity to enhance your mood, and seek support from trusted friends or family when necessary. Finally, reflect on this question: How can understanding and managing your emotions enhance your relationships and overall well-being?

Emotional Intelligence and Its Importance

Emotional intelligence, often abbreviated as EI, is a vital skill that goes beyond simply recognizing emotions. It includes the ability to identify, understand, and manage both your own feelings and those of others. This capability consists of several key components: self-awareness, self-regulation, motivation, empathy, and social skills. Each element plays a significant role in how you engage with your environment and interact with others.

Self-awareness acts as the foundation of emotional intelligence. It involves being keenly aware of your emotions as they arise and understanding how they affect your thoughts and behaviors. For instance, recognizing feelings of anxiety before an important exam allows you to acknowledge this emotion and assess its potential impact on your performance. Understanding your emotional state enables you to apply strategies for effective management, such as practicing relaxation techniques or reframing your thoughts.
Self-regulation describes the ability to control or redirect disruptive emotions and impulses. This skill allows you to pause and reflect before reacting and to calm yourself during distressing moments. For example, in a heated

disagreement with a friend, self-regulation gives you the opportunity to take a moment to breathe deeply and respond thoughtfully instead of reacting impulsively with anger. This ability is crucial for nurturing healthy relationships and reducing unnecessary conflicts.

Motivation, within the context of emotional intelligence, refers to the internal drive to pursue goals for personal fulfillment rather than seeking external validation. It involves a genuine passion for your pursuits and a commitment to self-improvement. For example, if you are driven to master a new skill, such as playing a musical instrument, you are more likely to practice consistently and navigate obstacles effectively, even when challenges arise.

Empathy represents the ability to understand and resonate with the emotions of others. This skill requires you to adopt another person's perspective and grasp their feelings. It is essential for building meaningful relationships, as it allows you to connect with others on a deeper level. When a friend faces difficulties, showing empathy through active listening and support can significantly enhance their emotional experience and foster a sense of belonging.

Social skills encompass the abilities necessary for effective interaction with others, including communication, conflict resolution, and teamwork. Strong social skills help establish and maintain relationships, whether with peers, family members, or colleagues. For instance, clear communication and active listening can reduce misunderstandings and strengthen your connections.

Emotional intelligence benefits not only personal relationships but also plays a crucial role in improving academic performance. It fosters focus, self-discipline, and adaptability, equipping you to handle new challenges and situations in an educational setting. For example, when facing difficulties in a particular subject, emotional intelligence helps you maintain motivation, manage stress levels, and proactively seek assistance when needed.

To enhance your emotional intelligence, consider engaging in specific exercises. Practicing active listening, where you fully concentrate on another person's words without interruption, can improve your empathy and social skills. Scenarios designed to build empathy, such as reflecting on how a character in a story might feel, can deepen your understanding of others' emotions. Activities like journaling about your emotional responses and behaviors can strengthen your self-awareness and self-regulation.

Real-world examples highlight the positive effects of emotional intelligence. For instance, a student who uses self-regulation to stay composed during a group project can facilitate more effective collaboration, leading to a superior final product. Alternatively, think of a friend who shows empathy by supporting a classmate who feels isolated, thereby reinforcing their relationship and creating a more inclusive atmosphere.

Finding a balance between expressing emotions and responding thoughtfully is crucial in social interactions. While it is important to communicate your feelings authentically, considering the potential impact of your words and actions on others is equally vital. Regularly practicing emotional intelligence skills in daily life can lead to more fulfilling relationships and improved academic outcomes.

To track your progress, use self-assessment tools such as mood journals or reflective questions. These resources can help you identify areas for improvement and recognize your achievements. As you continue to develop your emotional intelligence, it will become an invaluable asset for navigating the complexities of adolescence and beyond.

Identifying and Expressing Your Feelings

Try keeping an emotion diary for a week! Write down what you feel and why each day. This simple habit can help you spot patterns, understand your triggers, and make it easier to talk about your emotions with friends or family. The more you practice naming your feelings, the better you'll get at managing them and building stronger relationships.

Naming and recognizing your feelings is a crucial first step in effectively managing emotions. Accurately identifying what you're feeling makes processing those emotions and responding constructively significantly easier. Think of emotions as a specific vocabulary; without knowing the terms, effective communication becomes challenging. Learning to label your emotions enhances your ability to articulate feelings clearly, minimizing the risk of misunderstandings with others.

Let's explore some common emotions and their precise definitions to help you identify what you might be experiencing. Happiness involves a sense of joy or contentment, often accompanied by physical expressions like smiling or laughter. Sadness appears as a feeling of sorrow or unhappiness, which may lead to crying or a desire to withdraw from social interactions. Anger is characterized by annoyance or hostility, frequently resulting in physical responses such as a raised voice or muscle tension. Fear stems from the perception of danger, often causing physiological reactions like a racing heart or sweaty palms. Surprise brings an immediate feeling of astonishment, which can be either positive or negative, typically resulting in a gasp or widened eyes. Lastly, disgust represents a strong feeling of revulsion or disapproval, often prompting physical reactions like wrinkling your nose or turning away.

To boost emotional awareness, consider keeping a daily emotion diary. Each day, document specific events and your emotional responses to them. For instance, if you felt anxiety before a test, note the specific triggers and describe how it impacted you both physically and mentally. Over time, this practice will deepen your awareness and help you identify patterns in your emotional responses.

Labeling emotions accurately can significantly alleviate distress. When you can name what you're feeling, addressing the underlying causes and finding constructive ways to manage it becomes easier. For example, if you recognize feeling overwhelmed, you can implement strategies to manage your workload more effectively or seek support from colleagues or friends. This clarity can prevent misunderstandings and enhance interactions with others.

Expressing emotions constructively is another essential skill. One effective technique involves using 'I' statements, which emphasize your feelings rather than placing blame. For example, instead of saying, "You never listen to me," you might say, "I feel ignored when I'm not heard." This approach promotes open communication and reduces defensiveness. Active listening is also vital; it requires fully concentrating on what the other person is saying without interruptions, fostering understanding and empathy.

Role-playing scenarios can serve as an engaging and practical method to practice expressing feelings healthily. You can collaborate with friends or family by taking turns acting out various situations and discussing appropriate responses. For instance, you might role-play a disagreement with a friend and practice using 'I' statements and active listening techniques to resolve the conflict.

Mindfulness practices, such as deep breathing and meditation, play a key role in achieving emotional clarity and calmness. When feeling overwhelmed, taking slow, deep breaths can help regulate your nervous system and provide a moment to gather your thoughts. Engaging in meditation, even for just a few minutes each day, can enhance your awareness of emotions and improve your ability to manage them effectively.

Creating an emotion wheel can be a helpful visual tool for identifying and categorizing feelings. Draw a circle and divide it into sections, each representing a different emotion. As you experience various feelings, add them to the corresponding section of the wheel. This exercise can expand your emotional vocabulary and facilitate clearer self-expression.

Gratitude journaling is another impactful activity. Each day, write down several things you are thankful for, focusing on positive emotions and experiences. This practice can shift your perspective and enhance overall emotional well-being.

Chapter 3: Building Confidence and Self-Esteem

Confidence and self-esteem are closely related yet distinct concepts that play a crucial role in personal development. Confidence refers to the belief in your abilities to accomplish tasks and effectively face challenges, while self-esteem encompasses your overall sense of self-worth or personal value derived from achievements and qualities. Although they differ, an increase in confidence can enhance self-esteem, and a healthy level of self-esteem can foster greater confidence. Recognizing these concepts is essential for personal growth and success, as they significantly influence how you perceive yourself and interact with others in various contexts.

Self-belief serves as a cornerstone of personal development. It empowers you to take on new challenges, pursue goals, and overcome obstacles that may arise. A strong belief in your capabilities increases the likelihood of taking calculated risks and stepping outside your comfort zone, where substantial growth occurs. Positive self-talk shapes your self-image in powerful ways. The way you communicate with yourself can significantly impact both confidence and self-esteem. Negative self-talk, such as doubting your abilities or fixating on perceived flaws, can undermine your self-worth. In contrast, positive affirmations reinforce your strengths and capabilities, helping you cultivate a more constructive self-image.

To identify negative self-talk patterns, closely monitor your inner dialogue. Pay attention to moments when you criticize yourself or question your abilities. Once you recognize these patterns, challenge them by evaluating whether they are based on objective facts or unfounded assumptions. Transform negative thoughts into positive affirmations. For instance, if you find yourself thinking, "I'm not good at this," reframe it as, "I am learning and improving every day." This shift in perspective can gradually enhance your confidence and self-esteem.

Try this: Write a daily affirmation or positive statement about yourself. Each morning, take a moment to reflect on a specific quality or achievement you are proud of. Document it and repeat it to yourself throughout the day. This practice can help reinforce a positive self-image and incrementally boost your confidence over time.

Setting realistic goals serves as another effective strategy for building confidence. Achieving these goals provides a tangible sense of accomplishment and reinforces your belief in your abilities. Start by identifying a specific, achievable goal, such as completing a project or learning a new skill. Break it down into smaller, manageable steps, and systematically track your progress. Celebrate each milestone, regardless of its size, as it brings you closer to your ultimate objective. This process builds confidence and cultivates a sense of purpose and direction in your endeavors.

A growth mindset is key to enhancing self-esteem. This mindset involves viewing challenges as opportunities for learning and growth rather than as insurmountable obstacles. Adopting a growth mindset makes you more resilient in the face of setbacks and more willing to take on new challenges. Real-world examples of individuals who have overcome self-doubt to achieve success can be particularly inspiring. Consider the story of J.K. Rowling, who faced numerous rejections before successfully publishing the Harry Potter series. Her persistence and unwavering belief in her work ultimately led to worldwide success, illustrating the power of resilience and self-belief.

Engaging in activities that push you outside your comfort zone can also enhance social confidence. Joining clubs or teams provides structured opportunities to interact with others, develop new skills, and foster a sense of belonging. These experiences significantly enhance your confidence in social situations and facilitate the formation of meaningful connections.

Body language plays a significant role in projecting confidence. Maintaining eye contact, standing tall, and adopting an open posture effectively convey self-assurance to others and reinforce your own sense of confidence. Practice these techniques in everyday interactions to cultivate a more confident presence.

Positive Self-Talk for Confidence and Empowerment

Imagine having a unique ability that can significantly change how you see yourself and the world around you. This skill, known as positive self-talk, serves as a strategic tool to boost confidence and transform negative thoughts into constructive ones. It's the internal dialogue you maintain with yourself, which can greatly influence your emotions and behaviors. When utilized effectively, this ability allows you to shift your mindset and approach challenges with greater self-assurance.

Self-talk acts as the ongoing mental commentary accompanying you throughout your daily activities. It can either uplift and motivate or become a source of criticism and discouragement. The key to using it effectively lies in self-awareness—recognizing when thoughts turn negative and understanding how they affect your emotional state and actions. By improving your awareness of thought patterns, you can identify the negative thoughts that hinder your progress.
To start this process, consider keeping a journal to capture your thoughts as they arise. Each time you notice a negative thought, write it down. This practice helps track your progress and allows you to recognize patterns in your thinking. For example, if you often think, "I'm not good enough," jot it down. Over time, you will begin to see how frequently these thoughts occur and the specific situations in which they arise.

Once you identify negative thoughts, the next step involves reframing them into positive affirmations. This means changing a negative statement into a positive one that highlights your strengths and potential. For instance, if you catch yourself thinking, "I can't do this," reframe it as, "I am capable of learning and improving." Using "I am" statements is an effective strategy because it reinforces your identity and emphasizes your abilities.

Here's a "Try This" activity to help you practice reframing negative thoughts. Below are several common negative thoughts along with suggested positive alternatives:

- Negative: "I'm not smart enough."

  Positive: "I am always learning and growing."
- Negative: "I always mess things up."

  Positive: "I am capable of doing my best and learning from mistakes."

- Negative: "Nobody likes me."

  Positive: "I am a kind and caring person, and I am worthy of friendship."

Visualization serves as another technique to strengthen positive self-talk. This involves mentally picturing yourself successfully overcoming a challenge. Close your eyes and imagine being in a situation where you feel confident and competent. Visualize the specific steps you take and the positive outcome you achieve. This mental rehearsal can boost confidence and prepare you for real-life situations.

Establishing new thought habits requires consistency and repetition. Set aside specific time each day to practice positive self-talk. You might choose to include this practice in your morning routine or as part of your bedtime ritual. Creating a personal mantra or affirmation that resonates with you can act as a mental anchor during challenging times. For example, "I am strong and resilient" can serve as a powerful reminder of your inner strength.

When reflecting on a negative thought you often encounter, think about how to turn it into a positive one. By consistently applying these techniques, you will develop a more empowering inner dialogue that boosts your confidence and helps you navigate life's challenges with greater ease.

Overcoming Self-Doubt in Everyday Life

Whenever you catch yourself doubting your abilities, pause and take a deep breath. Remind yourself that everyone—even adults—feels unsure sometimes. Try writing down one thing you did well today, no matter how small. Over time, these positive notes can help you see your strengths more clearly and boost your confidence. Remember, progress is made one step at a time, and self-kindness is just as important as hard work.

Self-doubt refers to a feeling of uncertainty about one's abilities or worth, significantly affecting both confidence and self-esteem. For a 13-year-old, this feeling can pop up in various situations, like at school when tackling a tricky math problem that requires critical thinking and problem-solving skills, during social interactions when trying to strike up conversations with peers, or when setting personal goals like mastering a new instrument that calls for consistent practice and dedication. Experiencing self-doubt can make these situations feel overwhelming, leading to hesitation and a reluctance to take risks or explore new opportunities, which can hold back personal growth and development.

Common triggers for teens include the fear of failure, making new experiences feel a bit daunting. Comparing oneself to others, especially on social media where curated highlights of peers' successes are the norm, can amplify feelings of inadequacy. Watching classmates excel in areas where one struggles can lead to negative self-talk and a diminished sense of self-worth. Internalizing criticism from teachers, parents, or peers can also contribute to self-doubt, reinforcing the belief that expectations are not being met.

Self-reflection serves as a powerful tool to combat self-doubt. Analyzing specific instances where it arises allows teens to understand the underlying causes. Keeping a journal or thought log can be particularly beneficial. Documenting moments of self-doubt, along with the associated thoughts and feelings, can reveal patterns. This practice helps in identifying triggers and provides a space to critically evaluate the validity of these doubts. Are they based in reality, or are they founded on unfounded assumptions? Is there tangible evidence that contradicts these negative beliefs?

Mindfulness offers another effective strategy for managing self-doubt. Remaining present and focusing on the current moment helps reduce the anxiety that often tags along. Mindfulness practices, such as deep breathing exercises or guided meditation, can calm the mind and foster a sense of inner peace, making it easier to confront and challenge negative thoughts.

Overcoming self-doubt involves setting realistic, achievable goals and celebrating small accomplishments. Breaking down larger tasks into manageable steps allows teens to experience a sense of achievement with each milestone reached. This approach boosts confidence and reinforces belief in one's capabilities. Practicing self-compassion is equally important. Being kind to oneself, especially during moments of failure or setback, can prevent a spiral of negative self-talk and promote a healthier self-image.

Chapter 5: Smart Goal Setting

Setting goals is like crafting a clear roadmap for your aspirations. Without a well-defined target, it's all too easy to lose focus and direction. This is where the concept of SMART goals comes into play. SMART stands for Specific, Measurable, Achievable, Relevant, and Time-bound. These criteria help turn vague dreams into actionable plans, guiding you toward both personal and academic success.

Let's dive into each component of SMART goals. **Specific** means your goal should be clearly defined and straightforward. Instead of saying, "I want to do better in school," a specific goal would be, "I want to raise my math grade from a B to an A by the end of the semester." This clarity allows you to channel your efforts effectively. **Measurable** involves setting criteria to track your progress. For the math goal, you could measure improvement by checking test scores or monitoring homework grades. This approach helps you see how close you are to reaching your goal. **Achievable** ensures that your goal is realistic and attainable. While aiming high is commendable, setting a goal like "I want to become a math genius overnight" isn't practical. Instead, focus on what you can genuinely achieve with dedicated effort and the resources at your disposal. **Relevant** means your goal should be meaningful and align with your broader academic and personal objectives. If improving your math grade is crucial for gaining admission to a reputable high school or college, it becomes even more significant. Finally, **Time-bound** sets a deadline for your goal. This creates a sense of urgency and helps reduce procrastination. For example, aiming to improve your math grade by the end of the semester gives you a clear timeframe for your efforts.

Breaking long-term goals into short-term objectives is essential for effective progress. If your long-term goal is to improve your math grade, short-term objectives could include studying for one hour each day, attending weekly extra help sessions, or completing a specific number of additional practice problems each week. These smaller steps make the larger goal feel more manageable and less daunting.

Writing down your goals is a powerful strategy to boost commitment and accountability. Documenting them makes your objectives more tangible and concrete. Consider using a goal-setting journal or a digital application to track your progress. These tools can help you reflect on your achievements and adjust your strategies as needed.

Prioritizing among multiple goals is also important. Trying to achieve too many objectives at once can lead to burnout. Focus on a few key goals that resonate with your personal values and interests. This alignment enhances motivation and simplifies the commitment process.

Experiencing setbacks is a natural part of the goal-setting journey. When you encounter obstacles, view them as opportunities for learning and growth rather than sources of discouragement. Adjust your goals as necessary, but keep your eyes on the desired outcome. Flexibility is key to maintaining momentum.

Here's a "Try This" activity: Identify a personal interest or hobby you want to improve. Set a SMART goal related to it. For instance, if you enjoy playing the guitar, your goal could be, "I want to learn to play three new songs by the end of the month." Break this down into actionable steps: practice for 30 minutes daily, focus on one song each week, and assess your progress every Sunday. Write down your goal and track your progress in a journal or app.

Setting Realistic and Achievable Goals

When setting a goal, make it personal and meaningful to you—this will keep you motivated even when things get tough. If you ever feel stuck, don't be afraid to adjust your plan or ask for help. Remember, progress is more important than perfection! Celebrate each small win, and use setbacks as learning opportunities. Keeping a journal or using an app to track your steps can make your journey more fun and rewarding.

Setting goals involves a structured process that begins with identifying what truly matters to you. For instance, if you have a passion for drawing and want to enhance your skills, this personal interest will serve as a powerful motivator, helping you stay dedicated to your growth. The first step is to clearly articulate your aim. Instead of vaguely saying you want to "get better at drawing," specify it, such as "I want to create a detailed portrait by the end of the month." This clarity provides you with a concrete target and transforms your goal into something measurable.

Once you have a specific aim, break it down into smaller, manageable tasks. This approach helps you avoid feeling overwhelmed and allows you to focus on one task at a time. For example, if your goal is to create a portrait, you might start by practicing individual facial features, then move on to mastering shading techniques, and finally combine these skills into a complete drawing. Each task should have a set timeline, enabling you to track your progress and make adjustments as needed.

Flexibility plays a crucial role in the goal-setting process. Life can throw unexpected challenges your way, and you may need to revise your plans. If you find that a certain technique is harder than expected, be ready to adjust your timeline or approach. This adaptability ensures that setbacks won't derail your progress and allows you to keep moving forward.

Take the example of Alex, a 13-year-old who wanted to improve his math grades. He set a specific goal to raise his grade from a C to a B by the end of the semester. Alex divided this aim into smaller, actionable tasks: reviewing class notes for 20 minutes each day, completing an extra five practice problems weekly, and attending a one-hour tutoring session every Saturday. He also created a timeline for each task, such as spending 30 minutes daily on practice problems. By staying flexible, Alex could adjust his study schedule when unexpected events arose, ensuring he remained on track for improvement.

Recognizing potential obstacles is an essential part of the goal-setting process. Think about what might hinder your progress and come up with strategies to tackle these challenges. For Alex, distractions at home were an issue, leading him to choose a quiet library as his study spot. By anticipating these barriers, you can develop effective strategies to overcome them, increasing your chances of success.

Maintaining motivation is crucial for reaching your goals. Celebrate small achievements along the way to keep your spirits high. Each time you complete a task, take a moment to acknowledge your progress. This positive reinforcement boosts your confidence and encourages you to keep going. Keeping a progress log is another effective way to stay motivated. Documenting your advancements helps you visualize how far you've come and offers opportunities for reflection. You can use a journal or a digital app to track milestones and adjust your plan as needed.

Here are the key steps to setting and achieving your goals:

- Choose a goal that aligns with your interests or values

- Define your goal clearly and specifically

- Break the goal into smaller, actionable tasks

- Establish a timeline for each task

- Stay flexible and adaptable

- Identify potential obstacles and brainstorm solutions

- Celebrate small achievements to maintain motivation

- Keep a progress log to track milestones and reflect on your progress

Try This: Think of a personal interest or skill you want to improve. Set a specific goal related to it and break it down into smaller tasks. Create a timeline for each task and identify potential obstacles. Write down your plan and track your progress in a journal or app. Reflect on how breaking down your goal into steps makes it feel more achievable.

Reflection Question: How does breaking down your goals into smaller steps change your perspective on achieving them?

Tracking Progress and Celebrating Milestones

Monitoring progress towards goals is like using a trusty navigation tool that keeps you on track with your objectives. Regular assessments of performance are key to ensuring you're making effective strides and optimizing your efforts. This systematic evaluation not only fuels your motivation but also allows for necessary tweaks to your strategies, helping you stay efficient as you work towards your targets.

To track progress effectively, setting up a structured system is essential. There are various tools at your disposal, each with its own unique perks. A journal is a classic yet powerful method, providing a tangible space to document your achievements, challenges, and reflections. By recording specific accomplishments, like completed tasks or milestones reached, you gain a clear snapshot of your current status. This practice also encourages deeper reflection on your experiences, leading to valuable insights. On the other hand, digital applications offer a modern twist, often packed with features like reminders, progress analytics, and customizable goal-setting templates. These apps can be accessed on your smartphone or computer, making it easy to update your progress no matter where you are. A calendar, whether digital or paper, can also be a fantastic organizational tool. Marking important deadlines and milestones helps you visualize your timeline and stick to your schedule.

Being honest with yourself during evaluations is essential. It's easy to overlook areas that need improvement, but recognizing these challenges is the first step toward growth. Acknowledge when a plan needs a little adjustment and be ready to implement changes. This might involve setting more realistic goals, revising timelines, or seeking additional resources or support. Remember, the goal of monitoring progress is not to criticize yourself but to ensure you're on the right path and making the most of your efforts.

When progress seems to stall, adjusting your plans effectively is crucial to regain momentum. This requires a thoughtful evaluation of current strategies and a willingness to make changes that align with your specific objectives. Start by pinpointing the exact areas where challenges arise. Is it a matter of time management, a lack of resources, or perhaps a dip in motivation? Once you've accurately identified the problem, consider revising your timeline or breaking goals into smaller, more manageable tasks. This approach reduces the overwhelming nature of the goal and clarifies the steps needed to move forward.
Flexibility and an open mindset are essential for adapting plans. Sometimes, the initial strategy may not yield the best results, and that's perfectly okay. Being open to alternative methods can lead to innovative solutions and better outcomes. For instance, if sticking to a study schedule proves difficult, try experimenting with different techniques or environments. You might discover that studying in shorter, focused intervals with scheduled breaks enhances retention and engagement more effectively than lengthy, uninterrupted

sessions. Small adjustments like these can significantly boost productivity and keep your motivation high.

Recognizing milestones plays a vital role in sustaining motivation. Acknowledging both significant and minor achievements reinforces positive behavior and persistence. When you reach a milestone, take a moment to appreciate your efforts. This could involve treating yourself to a favorite snack, taking a break to engage in a hobby, or sharing your success with friends and family. Celebrations don't have to be elaborate; the key is to ensure they hold personal significance. Doing so creates a positive feedback loop that fosters ongoing effort and commitment.

Setbacks are an inherent part of any process. Instead of viewing them as failures, see them as opportunities for learning and growth. Adjusting plans does not mean abandoning goals; it represents a strategic and resilient approach to overcoming challenges. For example, if you find that a particular goal is no longer relevant or attainable, feel free to revise it. This may involve setting a new target or extending your timeline to accommodate unexpected circumstances. The ability to adapt is a crucial skill that will serve you well in various aspects of life.
To adjust plans effectively, consider these strategies:

1. **Reassess Your Goals**: Regularly evaluate objectives to ensure they remain relevant and achievable. If needed, modify them to better align with your current situation and available resources.

2. **Break Down Tasks**: Divide larger goals into smaller, actionable steps. This makes it easier to track progress and maintain momentum.
3. **Stay Flexible**: Be open to trying new approaches and techniques. What worked in the past may not always be the best solution for the present.

4. **Celebrate Achievements**: Acknowledge and reward yourself for reaching milestones, regardless of their size. This reinforces positive behavior and sustains motivation.

5. **Seek Support**: Don't hesitate to reach out to friends, family, or mentors for guidance and encouragement. They can offer valuable insights and help you stay focused.

Chapter 6: Study Skills and Learning Strategies

Effective study skills are essential for achieving academic success and fostering personal growth. These skills not only enhance your performance in educational settings but also equip you with strategies to tackle challenges in various areas of life. A solid understanding of these skills can significantly improve your learning experience, making it both more effective and enjoyable.

To enhance your study skills, the first step is to identify your unique learning style. Everyone processes information differently, and knowing your preferred method can greatly boost your efficiency. The four main styles are visual, auditory, reading/writing, and kinesthetic. Visual learners thrive when they can see information presented through diagrams, charts, and videos. If visual aids help you remember better, you likely identify as a visual learner. On the other hand, auditory learners grasp information best through listening, often preferring lectures, discussions, or audio recordings. If you find it easier to recall information from what you hear rather than what you read, this may be your dominant style. Reading/writing learners excel with textual information, favoring reading and note-taking as their primary ways of processing knowledge. If engaging with written content enhances your understanding, this could be your main style. Lastly, kinesthetic learners benefit from hands-on experiences, preferring to engage in activities and experiments. If you understand concepts better through physical interaction, you might be a kinesthetic learner. Identifying your learning style allows you to tailor techniques to match your strengths, thereby boosting your productivity.

Active learning is another effective strategy for enhancing study skills. This approach involves interacting with the material rather than passively consuming information. Techniques such as summarizing content, teaching peers, and applying knowledge to real-world scenarios can significantly improve your understanding and retention. Summarizing requires distilling information into your own words, reinforcing comprehension. Teaching others is particularly beneficial, as it necessitates clear explanations of concepts, ensuring a solid grasp of the material. Applying knowledge to real-life situations enhances relevance and memorability, linking abstract ideas to practical experiences.

Your study environment plays a significant role in your ability to concentrate and retain information. Creating a dedicated space can greatly enhance your focus and productivity. This area should be free from distractions and equipped with all necessary materials. A tidy workspace minimizes interruptions and allows for sustained concentration on tasks. Organizing your materials is also essential. Keep notes, textbooks, and supplies systematically arranged for easy access when needed. This organization saves time and reduces stress, as you won't need to search frantically for essential items.

Time management is a critical component of effective study skills. Using planners or digital tools to schedule sessions helps you allocate your time efficiently and ensures comprehensive coverage of all necessary material. Setting specific, measurable, attainable, relevant, and time-bound (SMART) goals provides both structure and motivation. For example, instead of a vague goal like "study math," a SMART goal would be "complete three algebra practice problems by 5 PM." This clarity aids in maintaining focus and tracking your progress.

Breaking down large tasks into smaller, manageable components is another strategy that can alleviate stress and enhance concentration. Tackling a significant project can feel overwhelming, but dividing it into smaller, actionable steps makes it more manageable. For instance, if you have a research paper due, you might segment the process into stages such as selecting a topic, conducting research, creating an outline, drafting, and revising. Each step acts as a mini-goal, making the overall task less intimidating and more achievable.

Different subjects often require distinct study strategies to maximize understanding and retention. For instance, mathematics and the sciences benefit significantly from engaging in problem-solving exercises and applying theoretical concepts through practice problems, while history and literature typically necessitate extensive reading and critical analysis of texts. Tailoring your approach to the specific demands of each subject can really enhance the effectiveness of your study sessions. A powerful technique to improve memory retention across all subjects is retrieval practice. This method involves actively recalling information from memory rather than passively reviewing notes or textbooks. Regularly testing yourself on the material—using methods such as flashcards, practice quizzes, or teaching the content to a peer—reinforces neural pathways associated with that information, thereby boosting your ability to retrieve it when necessary.

Another effective method to boost productivity is the Pomodoro Technique. This strategy segments study time into focused intervals, typically lasting 25 minutes, followed by a 5-minute break. After completing four of these intervals, take a longer break of 15 to 30 minutes. This structured approach helps maintain concentration and reduces the risk of burnout by giving your brain regular rest periods. It's particularly useful for managing large tasks by breaking them down into smaller, more manageable segments.

When it comes to note-taking, selecting a method that aligns with your learning style is essential. The Cornell Method divides notes into three sections: a narrow left column designated for cues or questions, a wider right column for detailed notes, and a summary section at the bottom. This format promotes active engagement with the material and enhances the efficiency of your review process. Alternatively, mind mapping serves as a visual technique that creates a diagram to represent information hierarchically. This method is especially advantageous for visual learners, as it organizes complex information in a way that is both comprehensible and memorable.

Group study sessions can also be highly beneficial, providing opportunities for collaborative learning and exposure to diverse perspectives. However, balancing these sessions with individual study time is crucial to ensure a comprehensive understanding of the material. Group studies clarify doubts and reinforce learning through discussion, while personal study time allows for deeper reflection and assimilation of concepts.

Effective Note-Taking Strategies

Effective note-taking is a vital skill that can significantly boost your ability to retain and organize information. In academic settings, using structured systems is key to accurately capturing and reviewing important details. Let's dive into some of the most effective methods to enhance your academic performance.

The outline method organizes information in a clear and hierarchical format. Start by jotting down the main topics as headings. Under each heading, add subtopics and specific details that relate to the main idea. This technique shines particularly in subjects with extensive content, like history or literature. Breaking the material into smaller, manageable components helps you clearly identify the relationships between various pieces of information. This structured approach not only facilitates comprehension but also simplifies the review process.

Another effective strategy is the charting method, which is perfect for subjects that require comparisons, such as science or social studies. In this approach, you create a table with defined columns and rows to systematically organize information. Each column represents a distinct category, while each row contains specific details relevant to that category. For example, when studying different animal species, you might create columns for habitat, diet, and lifespan, with rows dedicated to each species. This visual format allows for quick comparisons, making it easier to spot patterns and differences.

The sentence method works well for capturing detailed information rapidly, especially during fast-paced lectures. In this approach, you record each new piece of information as a separate sentence. Although it is less structured than the outline or charting techniques, it enables quick documentation without the immediate need for organization. You can later review your notes and reorganize them into a more structured format if necessary.

Color-coding serves as a powerful technique for categorizing information and enhancing visual memory. Assign distinct colors to specific topics or types of information to create a visual framework that aids in recalling details. For instance, you might designate one color for definitions, another for examples, and a third for significant dates. This method not only enhances the visual appeal of your notes but also makes it easier to locate specific information during review sessions.

Using symbols and abbreviations can streamline the note-taking process and improve efficiency. Develop a consistent set of symbols and shorthand that you can apply uniformly. For example, use an arrow to indicate a cause-and-effect relationship or an asterisk to highlight critical points. Abbreviations can also speed up your writing; for instance, use "w/" for "with" or "b/c" for "because." The key is to establish a system that you understand and can consistently apply across all your notes.

Reviewing and revising your notes shortly after class is vital for reinforcing memory retention. This practice solidifies the information in your mind and allows you to address any gaps or clarify points that were unclear during the lecture. Set aside time each day to review your notes, summarize key points, and make necessary adjustments. This habit not only enhances your understanding but also prepares you for upcoming exams and assignments.

In today's digital landscape, numerous tools and applications are available to help you organize and securely store your notes. Digital note-taking applications like Evernote, OneNote, or Google Keep offer features such as cloud storage, search capabilities, and the option to incorporate multimedia elements like images and audio recordings. These tools can be particularly beneficial for maintaining organized and accessible notes across various devices.

Professionals in various fields rely on effective note-taking to excel in their careers. For instance, journalists use shorthand to quickly capture quotes during interviews, while scientists keep detailed notes to document their experiments and findings. Cultivating strong skills enhances your ability to learn and retain information, establishing a solid foundation for future success. To practice different methods and find the one that suits you best, try each technique during your study sessions. Apply the outline method for one subject, the charting method for another, and the sentence method for a third. Observe which approach helps you understand and retain the material most effectively. You may discover that a combination of techniques works best for different subjects or types of information. As you refine your skills, you will gain confidence in your ability to capture and organize information efficiently.

Mind mapping serves as a fantastic tool for visual learners, providing a structured way to effectively organize and connect ideas. To create a mind map, start with a central concept placed prominently in the center of your page. From this core idea, draw branches that represent related topics or subtopics, making sure each branch is clearly labeled. Each branch can further split into smaller branches, capturing increasingly detailed information, such as definitions, examples, or key points. This method helps visualize the relationships between various pieces of information and boosts memory retention by engaging both the logical and creative sides of your thinking. Mind maps are especially helpful for subjects that require a deep understanding of complex systems or processes, like biology, where the interconnections among concepts are crucial, or history, where timelines and events are intertwined.

The Cornell Note-Taking System offers another effective method that greatly enhances the organization and review of notes. This system divides the page into three distinct sections: a narrow left column for cues or questions, a larger right column for detailed notes, and a summary section at the bottom. The left column, known as the recall column, is where you jot down keywords or questions that trigger the main ideas captured in your notes. This structured setup encourages active engagement with the material, making it easier to review and recall information later. After class, take some time to work on the summary section to condense the main points in your own words, reinforcing your understanding and aiding in long-term retention.

Incorporating multimedia elements into your notes can significantly enrich your learning experience. Audio recordings of lectures or discussions are a great resource for auditory learners, allowing them to revisit the material at their own pace and reinforce key concepts. Images, diagrams, and videos can also provide visual context and enhance comprehension. For instance, when studying a historical event, including a detailed timeline or a geographical map can help visualize the sequence of events and their spatial relationships. These multimedia elements blend seamlessly into digital notes, making them more interactive and engaging.

Test Preparation Tips and Study Strategies

Try using the Pomodoro Technique to boost your focus: study for 25 minutes, then take a 5-minute break. After four rounds, reward yourself with a longer break. This method helps prevent burnout and keeps your mind fresh, making study sessions more effective and less stressful.

Creating a personalized study schedule is essential for effective test and exam preparation. This approach helps you manage your time wisely, allowing you to cover all necessary material without feeling overwhelmed. Start by evaluating the time available until the test date. Mark the date on a calendar and calculate the exact number of days or weeks for preparation. This will give you a clear understanding of your timeframe, enabling you to strategically plan your study sessions.

After establishing a timeline, allocate time for each subject based on complexity and importance. List all subjects to study and rank them according to difficulty or the amount of material needing attention. For instance, if mathematics poses a particular challenge, consider dedicating 60% more study time to it compared to a subject like history, which may only need 30% of your total study time. This prioritization allows you to focus more on areas needing improvement, thereby increasing your chances of achieving a high score.

Dividing study sessions into manageable segments proves to be an effective strategy. Long, uninterrupted periods can lead to mental fatigue and decreased concentration. Instead, aim for shorter, focused sessions lasting 25 to 50 minutes, followed by regular breaks. This method enhances focus and improves information retention. A popular approach is the Pomodoro Technique, which involves studying for 25 minutes and then taking a 5-minute break. After completing four cycles, take a longer break of 15 to 30 minutes. This structured method helps maintain concentration and prevents burnout by providing necessary rest intervals.

Establishing specific times and quiet spaces for study is crucial for creating a consistent routine and minimizing distractions. Choose a time of day when you feel most alert and productive, whether it's early in the morning or later in the evening. Consistency is key, so try to stick to the same study times each day. Identify a quiet environment where you can focus without interruptions, such as a library, a dedicated study room, or a cozy corner in your home. Ensure this space is free from distractions like television or loud noises, and keep it organized with all necessary materials readily available.

Regular review sessions are vital for reinforcing material over time. Instead of cramming all the information at once, spread out your review sessions to revisit the material multiple times before the test. This spaced repetition technique strengthens memory and comprehension of the subject. For example, if you're preparing for a science exam, review your notes and key concepts every two to three days leading up to the test. This consistent reinforcement makes it easier to recall information when needed.

Using digital calendars or planners can significantly improve your ability to track progress and adjust your study schedule as needed. These tools allow you to set reminders for study sessions, deadlines, and review periods, helping you stay on track. Many digital planners also offer features like color-coding and task prioritization, which can help organize your study plan more effectively. For instance, you might use one color for math assignments and another for science, making it easy to identify focus areas for each day.

Successful students often structure their study time by setting specific goals for each session. Instead of vague objectives like "study history," they establish clear, measurable goals such as "review chapters 3 and 4 and complete five practice questions." This specificity provides direction and motivation, making it easier to assess progress. They also regularly evaluate their understanding of the material, identifying areas that require further review or practice. By remaining adaptable and willing to modify their study plan as necessary, they ensure consistent focus on the most critical tasks.

Active recall is a fantastic technique that can really boost both your retention and understanding of the material. This method involves actively testing yourself on what you've learned, rather than just passively going over notes or textbooks. By retrieving information from memory, you strengthen the neural connections tied to that knowledge, making it easier to recall during assessments. To put active recall into practice, consider using flashcards as a handy tool. Write a specific question or key concept on one side and the corresponding answer or explanation on the other. Make it a habit to quiz yourself regularly, especially on the areas where you find the most challenge. This practice not only solidifies your memory but also helps pinpoint topics that might need a little extra attention.

Practice tests and past exams are invaluable resources for getting comfortable with test formats and question types. They offer a realistic simulation of the exam environment, which can help you manage your time effectively and ease any anxiety. Engaging with these tests allows you to spot patterns in the types of questions asked and identify areas that might need more focus. After completing a practice test, take the time to review your answers thoroughly. Analyzing any mistakes helps you understand what went wrong and develop strategies for improvement. This reflective process is key for ongoing growth and building your confidence.

Summarizing key points and concepts on flashcards is another effective review strategy. This approach encourages you to condense information into concise, manageable pieces, which can enhance both understanding and retention. Use these cards for quick reviews, especially in the days leading up to an exam. Their portability makes them perfect for reinforcing knowledge during short breaks or while commuting.

Group study sessions create a collaborative environment where you can discuss challenging topics and gain diverse perspectives. Explaining concepts to peers requires a solid understanding, which in turn reinforces your own knowledge. These discussions can also uncover insights and strategies you might not have thought of before. When participating in a study group, aim to keep sessions focused and productive. Set clear objectives for each meeting and allocate specific time slots for each topic to keep discussions on track.

Using varied review methods is essential for achieving a well-rounded understanding. Teaching the material to someone else is an exceptionally effective strategy. This process requires you to organize your thoughts and articulate them clearly, reinforcing your grasp of the subject matter. Creating mind maps is another excellent technique, especially for visual learners. Mind maps allow you to visually structure information, illustrating the relationships between different concepts. This method helps you see the bigger picture and understand how individual pieces of information connect.

Chapter 7: Communication Skills for Everyday Life

Communication skills are a vital asset that can significantly enhance your ability to forge strong relationships and achieve success across various domains of life. Engaging in casual conversations with friends, collaborating on a group project, or interacting in online environments all require effective communication. Let's start with verbal communication, which includes the specific words you choose and how you articulate them. Speaking clearly, along with an appropriate tone and volume, greatly influences how your message is perceived. For example, if you are in a bustling cafeteria trying to share details about an exciting event, mumbling or speaking too softly may cause your friend to miss important information. On the flip side, raising your voice excessively could come across as confrontational. Finding the right balance is crucial to ensure your message is both heard and understood.

Active listening is another fundamental aspect of verbal communication. This skill involves fully engaging with what the other person is expressing instead of merely waiting for your turn to respond. You can show your engagement by maintaining consistent eye contact, nodding, and providing verbal affirmations like "I see" or "That makes sense." Demonstrating active listening conveys respect and genuine interest in the conversation, strengthening your rapport with others.

Non-verbal communication is equally important, encompassing body language, eye contact, and facial expressions. For instance, if you are telling a story and your friend is distracted by their phone, you might interpret that as a lack of interest, even if they are still listening. Similarly, crossing your arms can unintentionally signal defensiveness or a closed-off demeanor. Being aware of these non-verbal cues can enhance your ability to convey your message effectively and understand the feelings of others.

Empathy plays a critical role in effective communication. This involves understanding and acknowledging another person's feelings and perspectives. When you respond with empathy, you validate their emotions and show that you care. For example, if a friend expresses disappointment over a low test score, saying "I understand how disappointing that must be" can provide more comfort than simply offering solutions without acknowledgment.

Improving your listening skills can significantly enhance overall communication effectiveness. Practice maintaining eye contact and providing feedback during conversations. Try summarizing the key points of what the other person has said to confirm your understanding. This approach not only shows that you are attentive but also helps clarify any potential misunderstandings.

Asking open-ended questions fosters dialogue effectively. Instead of posing questions that can be answered with a simple "yes" or "no," opt for inquiries that encourage more elaborate responses. For example, rather than asking "Did you like the movie?" you could ask "What aspects of the movie resonated with you?" This method invites a more engaging and meaningful conversation.

Practicing assertive communication involves expressing your thoughts and feelings candidly while respecting the perspectives of others. This requires finding a middle ground between passivity and aggression. For instance, if a friend frequently arrives late, you might say, "I feel frustrated when we start late because I value our time together. Can we agree on a time that accommodates both of our schedules?" This approach establishes boundaries respectfully and promotes collaboration.

In today's digital landscape, communication extends beyond in-person interactions. Digital communication, whether through text messages, emails, or social media platforms, requires a distinct set of skills. Understanding netiquette, or online etiquette, is essential. This includes maintaining politeness, avoiding the use of all capital letters (which can be interpreted as shouting), and being mindful of your tone. Remember that without facial expressions or vocal inflections, written messages are prone to misinterpretation.

Active Listening and Clear Communication Skills

Effective communication is a vital skill that helps you forge meaningful connections with others, express your ideas clearly, and appreciate diverse perspectives. Active listening is one of the most important elements of communication. This means being fully engaged in conversations, which involves minimizing distractions and maintaining consistent eye contact. Focusing on the speaker shows that you value their input. You can achieve this by putting away your phone or turning off the television when someone is talking to you. Eye contact acts as a strong indicator of attention and respect, creating an environment where the speaker feels acknowledged and understood.
Improving your listening skills can also be accomplished through note-taking. While you don't need to write down every word, jotting down key points can help you retain important information and demonstrate your engagement. This technique proves especially useful in academic discussions or when receiving detailed instructions. It also prepares you to ask informed questions later, highlighting your attentiveness.
Providing verbal feedback plays a vital role in active listening. Summarizing or paraphrasing the speaker's message helps confirm understanding. For example, if a friend shares a challenge they are facing, you might respond with, "So, what you're saying is that you're feeling overwhelmed with your homework and need help managing your time?" This response shows that you are listening and helps clarify any potential misunderstandings.

Regulating emotions is crucial to avoid interruptions or impulsive reactions during conversations. While experiencing strong feelings is natural, mastering emotional control can help prevent misunderstandings and conflicts. Techniques like deep breathing or counting to ten before responding can help you maintain composure and focus. Empathy is also essential, as it involves recognizing and understanding the speaker's emotions and perspectives. Considering their viewpoint allows for more thoughtful and compassionate responses.
Engaging in practical exercises can further develop your active listening skills. One effective exercise is "mirroring," where you reflect the speaker's words back to them. This can involve repeating a key phrase or summarizing their main points. Mirroring ensures clarity and shows genuine interest in the message. Asking clarifying questions can deepen understanding and facilitate the flow of conversation. Questions like "Can you elaborate on that?" or "What do you mean by that?" encourage the speaker to provide further context.

Next, let's focus on clear speaking skills. Organizing your thoughts before speaking is essential for delivering messages concisely. Consider what you want to communicate and structure your ideas logically. A well-organized message is easier for listeners to follow and understand. Using pauses effectively can also enhance communication. Pauses give your audience time to process information and can emphasize significant points. They also provide a moment to gather your thoughts and ensure clarity in your message.

Varying your tone and pace is another strategy to keep listeners engaged. Speaking in a monotone voice can make your message uninteresting, while adjusting pitch and speed can make it more captivating. Non-verbal cues such as gestures and facial expressions significantly reinforce verbal messages. For instance, a smile can convey warmth, while a nod can indicate agreement or understanding.

Structuring conversations with a clear beginning, middle, and end enhances the coherence of your message. Start by presenting your main point, elaborate on it with supporting details, and conclude with a summary or a call to action. This structure helps your audience follow your reasoning and retain key points.

To practice these skills, consider participating in group activities or role-playing scenarios. These controlled environments provide a safe space to experiment with different communication styles and receive constructive feedback. For example, you might practice delivering a brief presentation to friends or family, focusing on organizing your thoughts and effectively using non-verbal cues.

Understanding Nonverbal Communication

Recognizing nonverbal cues involves mastering a rich communication system that relies on gestures, facial expressions, and body movements rather than spoken language. These signals can provide valuable insights into a person's emotions or thoughts, even when words are absent. For instance, crossing arms might suggest defensiveness or a need for personal space, while a genuine smile typically indicates friendliness and openness. By accurately identifying these cues, you can deepen your understanding of the emotions and intentions of those around you, making your interactions more impactful and effective.

Let's explore some common nonverbal cues. **Posture** is a fundamental component. Standing or sitting upright often conveys confidence and attentiveness, while slouching can imply disinterest or fatigue. **Gestures** also play a critical role in communication. For example, nodding signifies agreement or understanding, while repetitive fidgeting may reveal nervousness or impatience. **Eye contact** is vital for effective communication. Maintaining appropriate eye contact shows engagement and interest in the conversation. However, too much can come across as confrontational, while too little may suggest shyness or a lack of interest. **Facial expressions** rank among the most revealing nonverbal cues. A furrowed brow can indicate confusion or concern, while a relaxed expression typically reflects calmness or contentment.

It's important to remember that nonverbal cues can vary significantly across different cultures. A gesture that seems friendly in one culture might be seen as offensive in another. For example, in some cultures, direct eye contact is a sign of respect, while in others, it may be viewed as confrontational. Recognizing these cultural differences is essential for accurately interpreting signals. Observing and practicing the interpretation of these cues in everyday interactions can greatly enhance your ability to communicate effectively with people from diverse backgrounds.

Next, let's focus on how to use nonverbal cues to improve communication. **Open posture**, featuring uncrossed arms and legs, can make you seem more approachable and receptive. This is especially important in discussions where building trust is key. **Appropriate eye contact** can strengthen verbal messages and show that you are actively listening. When expressing empathy or understanding, your facial expressions can significantly affect the interaction. A warm smile or a nod can effectively convey genuine interest in what the speaker is saying.

Chapter 8: Healthy Relationships and Friendships

Healthy relationships form the foundation of a fulfilling life, offering support, trust, and mutual respect. These connections rely on several key characteristics that ensure they nurture and benefit everyone involved. **Mutual respect** stands out as a fundamental element, where each person values the other's opinions, feelings, and boundaries. This creates an environment where individuals feel safe to express themselves openly, allowing for honest dialogue without fear of judgment or ridicule.

Trust serves as another critical component, acting as the glue that holds relationships together. It involves a strong belief in the reliability and integrity of the other person, with the expectation that they will act in your best interest. Over time, trust develops through consistent actions, transparency, and honesty, which are essential for fostering a sense of security and stability.

Support plays an equally important role, encompassing the act of being present for one another during both positive and negative experiences. This includes actively offering encouragement during achievements, celebrating milestones, and providing emotional comfort during challenging times. Supportive relationships enhance individuals' feelings of being valued and understood, significantly contributing to their overall mental and emotional well-being.

Effective communication serves as the lifeline of any healthy relationship. It requires not only clear articulation of thoughts and feelings but also active listening to fully grasp the other person's perspective. This reciprocal exchange ensures that both parties feel acknowledged and understood, thereby reducing the likelihood of misunderstandings and conflicts.

Setting boundaries is vital for maintaining healthy relationships. They define acceptable behaviors and help protect personal space and individuality, ensuring that each person feels comfortable and respected, preventing feelings of being overwhelmed or taken for granted.

Empathy and understanding significantly contribute to fostering strong connections. Considering the other person's perspective and emotions deepens relational bonds and promotes a culture of compassion and kindness.

Healthy friendships and family relationships often feature open communication, shared interests, and mutual support. In a healthy friendship, both individuals feel at ease being their authentic selves, confident in the knowledge that they are accepted and appreciated for who they are. Family relationships thrive when love, respect, and open dialogue are balanced, allowing each member to feel valued and supported.

Positive relationships profoundly impact mental and emotional well-being. They provide a sense of belonging and security, effectively reducing feelings of loneliness and isolation. These connections can boost self-esteem, increase overall happiness, and even improve physical health by lowering stress levels.

Recognizing unhealthy relationships is crucial for maintaining well-being. Signs include manipulation, excessive control, and a lack of respect. **Manipulation** occurs when one person attempts to control or influence the other for their own benefit, often leading to feelings of guilt or obligation. **Excessive control** can manifest as one person dictating the other's actions, decisions, or social interactions, thereby stifling independence. A **lack of respect** is evident when one person's feelings, opinions, or boundaries are consistently disregarded or dismissed.

Reflecting on personal relationships provides a valuable opportunity to identify areas for improvement. Consider whether your connections exhibit mutual respect, trust, and support. Are there recurring patterns of behavior that need attention? Are there boundaries that require establishment or reinforcement? Taking the time to evaluate your relationships can lead to healthier, more fulfilling connections.

Maintaining healthy relationships demands ongoing effort and commitment. Regular communication is essential, ensuring that both parties stay connected and informed about each other's lives. **Active listening**, where you fully engage with what the other person is saying, strengthens the bond and shows that you value their input. Being present, both physically and emotionally, signifies your commitment and helps build trust.

Resolving conflicts calmly and respectfully is crucial for maintaining harmony. This involves addressing issues directly and honestly, without resorting to blame or criticism. Finding common ground and being willing to compromise can help resolve disagreements and strengthen the relationship. Practicing these skills in real-life situations, such as role-playing conflict resolution scenarios, can enhance your ability to navigate challenges effectively.

Expanding your social circle and meeting new people can be an exciting journey that opens up a world of opportunities for both personal and professional growth. Friendships are more than just fun; they play a crucial role in enhancing emotional well-being and cognitive development. To nurture new relationships, embrace openness to individuals from various backgrounds and experiences. This willingness not only enriches your life but also broadens your perspective, allowing for a deeper appreciation of different cultures and viewpoints.

Starting conversations can sometimes feel a bit daunting, especially for those who are shy or experience social anxiety. But don't worry—there are several strategies to make this process smoother. Look for common interests with others, whether it's a shared love for a specific sport, hobby, or even a favorite book or movie. Open-ended questions are a fantastic way to keep the conversation flowing. Instead of sticking to yes or no questions, ask about someone's experiences or opinions, which can lead to more engaging and meaningful discussions.

Getting involved in social activities, clubs, and online communities offers great opportunities to connect with peers. Joining a group that resonates with your interests not only fosters a sense of belonging but also makes it easier to meet like-minded individuals. Online communities, when approached safely and responsibly, can also be wonderful spaces to connect with others who share your passions, breaking down geographical barriers.

Promoting inclusivity and celebrating diversity in friendships is essential for creating a supportive and enriching social environment. Embrace the differences in others and appreciate the unique perspectives they bring. This mindset not only strengthens friendships but also nurtures a culture of acceptance and understanding.

Overcoming shyness or social anxiety takes practice and patience. Start with small, achievable goals, like introducing yourself to a new acquaintance or attending a social event. Gradually, these little steps can boost your confidence and make social interactions feel more natural. Remember, it's completely normal for everyone to feel nervous at times, and it's perfectly okay to move at your own pace.

To sharpen your social skills, think about joining a new group or attending a community event. These settings provide structured opportunities to engage with others, making it easier to practice conversation skills and build confidence. After each interaction, take a moment to reflect on what went well and pinpoint areas for improvement for future encounters.

Building Trust and Positive Friendships

Trust serves as the foundation of any meaningful friendship. It represents the belief that someone will act in your best interest, built through behaviors like honesty, reliability, and consistency. When you trust another person, you feel secure sharing your thoughts and feelings, confident that they will be respected and kept confidential. To be trustworthy, keeping promises, being punctual, and respecting confidences is crucial. If you commit to a task, make sure you follow through. This consistency in actions and words demonstrates dependability. Transparency and open communication play vital roles in building and maintaining trust. Being candid about your feelings and intentions, even when it feels a bit uncomfortable, helps create a strong bond. If a mistake occurs, acknowledge it and offer a sincere apology. This honesty reinforces trust and shows that you truly value the relationship.

Respect is another cornerstone of positive friendships. Valuing others' opinions, feelings, and boundaries is essential. Listening attentively when someone speaks, without interrupting or dismissing their thoughts, powerfully demonstrates respect. This behavior shows that you appreciate their perspective and are open to considering their point of view. Acknowledging feelings, even in disagreement, is also important. It reflects empathy and understanding, which are crucial for maintaining healthy relationships. Respectful behavior can significantly influence friendship dynamics, creating an environment where everyone feels valued and heard. When mistakes occur, offering a sincere apology is essential. It indicates that you recognize the impact of your actions and are committed to making amends.

Maintaining positive, supportive friendships requires effort and commitment. Being available in times of need, offering encouragement, and celebrating successes all contribute to providing support. When a friend faces a difficult period, being present to listen and offer a shoulder to lean on can make a significant difference. Empathy and understanding are crucial during these challenging times. Strive to understand their perspective and offer support that resonates with them. Mutual support strengthens bonds and fosters a sense of belonging. Celebrating successes, regardless of their size, is also important. This action shows that you are genuinely happy for your friend's achievements and are there to cheer them on.

Setting Boundaries and Assertive Communication

Boundaries serve as essential frameworks that define what is acceptable and comfortable in your interpersonal relationships. They play a critical role in friendships by protecting personal space, time, and emotional health. Think of them as specific guidelines about how you expect to be treated and how you will treat others in return. These guidelines help maintain a balance between fostering intimacy and preserving individuality. Without clear boundaries, friendships can become overwhelming, often leading to discomfort or resentment.
Different types of boundaries each serve a unique purpose. Emotional boundaries focus on safeguarding feelings and ensuring that your emotional landscape is respected. For example, if a friend often makes jokes that hurt you, it may be necessary to ask them directly to stop. Physical boundaries relate to personal space and comfort levels, which could mean telling a friend that you are uncomfortable with physical affection, like hugs, or that you need some time alone when feeling upset. Digital boundaries have become increasingly important in online interactions, involving limits on your availability for chats or deciding what personal information to share on social media.
Healthy boundaries in friendships include respecting each other's time by not expecting immediate replies to messages or recognizing when a friend needs time alone to recharge. While they can be flexible, boundaries should remain

firm regarding core values and what contributes to your sense of safety and respect. For instance, if honesty is a fundamental value, you might set a boundary that prohibits any form of dishonesty in friendships.

To identify personal boundaries, start with introspection. Pay attention to your emotional responses in different situations. Do you feel uneasy when a friend borrows your belongings without asking? Are you annoyed when someone interrupts you while speaking? These reactions can offer valuable insights into where your boundaries lie. Once identified, clearly and assertively communicate them.

Assertiveness means expressing needs and boundaries in a direct and respectful way. It involves standing up for yourself without being aggressive or passive. Using 'I' statements can be an effective strategy in assertive communication. For instance, instead of saying, "You never listen to me," you might say, "I feel unheard when I am interrupted." This approach highlights your feelings rather than placing blame. Maintaining eye contact and using a calm tone can further enhance the effectiveness of your message.

To practice establishing and communicating boundaries, engage in role-playing exercises with a friend or family member. For example, you could rehearse saying, "I need some time to myself right now," or "I am not comfortable with that joke." These sessions can help build confidence for real-life interactions.

Sometimes, others may test your boundaries. It is important to stay firm while remaining open to discussion. If a friend questions your boundary, take the chance to explain why it matters and be willing to listen to their perspective. This exchange can promote mutual understanding and respect for each other's needs.

Respecting others' boundaries is just as important as establishing your own. This practice fosters a sense of mutual respect and understanding within friendships. If a friend indicates that they need space, honoring that request shows that you value their comfort and emotional well-being.

Reflect on your current boundaries. Are there specific areas where you feel uncomfortable or disrespected? Consider what changes you might need to ensure your friendships remain healthy and balanced. This reflection can help you develop stronger, more respectful relationships.

Chapter 10: Making Good Decisions

Making decisions is a fundamental part of life, and the ability to make effective choices significantly influences personal success and overall well-being. At 13, you are at a developmental stage where you increasingly take responsibility for making decisions independently, whether related to academics, social relationships, or how to allocate your leisure time. Knowing how to make informed choices empowers you to approach these situations with confidence and clarity.

The decision-making process provides a systematic approach to assist in making well-informed choices. It starts with clearly identifying the decision that needs to be made, which involves recognizing a specific goal or problem. For example, you might need to determine whether to join a new club at school, which could enhance your social network and skill set, or how to spend your weekend in a way that balances relaxation and productivity. Clearly defining the decision establishes a solid foundation for the subsequent steps.

After identifying the decision, the next step involves gathering relevant information. This means seeking out credible sources and considering a variety of perspectives. For instance, if you're contemplating a new hobby, you might conduct online research, engage in discussions with friends who have experience in that area, or consult a teacher for guidance. Gathering information equips you with a comprehensive understanding of the available options and the potential outcomes associated with each choice.

Once you have collected information, identifying alternatives becomes essential. This step encourages brainstorming and creative thinking. Avoid limiting yourself to the most apparent choices; explore a wide range of possibilities. If you're deciding how to spend your summer, consider diverse activities, such as volunteering for a local organization, enrolling in a workshop to learn a new skill, or dedicating time to rest and recharge.

With a list of alternatives in hand, the next step involves weighing the evidence for each option. This requires systematically detailing the pros and cons of each choice. Assess how each option aligns with your personal values and long-term goals. For example, if one option offers significant opportunities for personal growth but requires a greater time commitment, evaluate that against an easier choice that may not provide the same level of fulfillment.

After evaluating the options, you need to select among them. This step requires focusing on what aligns best with your values and objectives. Trust your judgment and make a decision that resonates with you. Remember, there is rarely a flawless choice, but making a decision is preferable to remaining paralyzed by indecision.

Once a choice is made, the next step is to take action. Commit to your decision and execute it. Whether enrolling in a new class or initiating a project, taking action is essential to realizing the outcomes of your decision.

Finally, review the decision and its consequences. Reflect on what aspects were successful and what could have been approached differently. This step emphasizes learning opportunities and helps enhance decision-making skills for future scenarios.

Here's a "Try This" activity: Think of a decision you need to make, such as selecting an extracurricular activity or planning a weekend outing. Use the decision-making process outlined above to guide you. Identify the decision, gather information, list alternatives, weigh the pros and cons, make a choice, take action, and review the outcome. Reflect on how this process facilitated a more informed decision.

Making Thoughtful Decisions Every Day

When making decisions, try creating a simple pros and cons chart. Write down all the positives and negatives for each option, and then rank them by importance to you. This helps you see the big picture and makes it easier to choose what truly fits your goals and values. Don't forget to consider both short-term and long-term effects, and ask a trusted adult for advice if you feel stuck. Practicing this method will make tough choices less overwhelming!

Making thoughtful decisions requires a clear understanding of the pros and cons involved. These aspects highlight the specific positive and negative elements of a choice, serving as a systematic tool to evaluate various options. This approach is vital for informed decision-making, as it encourages consideration of all possible outcomes instead of relying on impulse or emotional reactions.

To weigh these factors effectively, start by defining the decision at hand. Once you have clarity on the matter, compile a comprehensive list of potential positive outcomes (pros) and negative outcomes (cons) associated with each option. Honesty and thoroughness are essential in this step. Examine every angle, including those that may not be immediately obvious. For example, if you are thinking about joining a new sports team, a pro might be improved physical fitness, while a con could be less time for academic assignments.

When listing pros and cons, consider both short-term and long-term effects. Immediate choices can lead to lasting consequences, so evaluate how each option might affect you now and in the future. For instance, choosing to spend time studying for a test might mean missing a social event with friends, but it could also result in better grades and more opportunities down the line.

Organizing your pros and cons can help clarify the decision-making process. One effective method is to create a table or chart. This visual representation allows you to see all the information at a glance, making it easier to compare the different aspects of each option. You can set up two columns, one for pros and one for cons, and categorize each point accordingly. This approach not only organizes your thoughts but also helps identify which factors are most significant in your decision.

Personal values and priorities play a significant role in evaluating these factors. What one person sees as a pro might be a con for someone else, depending on their unique values and priorities. For example, if you highly value academic success, the benefit of having extra study time may outweigh the drawback of missing a social gathering. Ranking the pros and cons based on their relevance to you can guide you in making a decision that aligns with your personal values and goals.

To practice this process, choose a decision you need to make, such as whether to take up a new hobby. List the pros and cons of this decision, considering both immediate and future impacts. For instance, a pro might be learning a new skill, while a con could be less available leisure time. After listing them, evaluate their impact on your life and rank them according to their importance. This exercise will help you understand how different factors influence your decision and how to prioritize them effectively.

Recognizing external influences, such as peer opinions, is also important, as they can distort your perception of pros and cons. Friends and family may have their own views on what you should do, but it's crucial to remain objective and focus on what matters most to you. To maintain objectivity, keep your personal values and goals in mind, and consider seeking advice from a trusted mentor or adult who can provide a balanced perspective. This way, you can ensure that your decision reflects your true self and is not overly influenced by others.

Considering consequences plays a crucial role in making informed decisions. This process involves forecasting the outcomes of your choices and understanding their potential impacts on your life and the lives of others. A thorough analysis of the possible results associated with each option is necessary. One effective way to anticipate consequences is to ask 'what if' questions. For example, you might wonder, 'What if I choose to dedicate my weekend to studying instead of socializing with friends?' or 'What if I decide to join the school debate team?' These inquiries help explore various scenarios and their potential ramifications.

When assessing consequences, evaluating both positive and negative outcomes in detail is essential. Positive results may include achieving specific academic or personal goals, acquiring new skills relevant to your career aspirations, or enhancing interpersonal relationships through collaboration. On the flip side, negative outcomes could involve missing out on alternative opportunities, experiencing increased stress levels, or facing unforeseen challenges. Weighing these factors systematically allows for more informed decisions that align with long-term objectives and core values. Long-term thinking is vital because today's choices can have lasting effects on your future. For instance, prioritizing studies may lead to improved academic performance and expanded opportunities for scholarships or internships, even if it means sacrificing some leisure activities in the short term.

Learning from Mistakes for Better Decisions

Reflecting on mistakes is a powerful tool for personal growth and informed decision-making. This process involves systematically reviewing past errors to understand the specific factors that contributed to the misstep and the underlying reasons, all while keeping a positive attitude towards yourself. Such reflection boosts self-awareness and resilience, allowing you to learn from experiences and make more informed choices in the future. A close examination helps identify recurring patterns, analyze the emotions involved, and refine strategies to prevent similar errors.

The first step in effective reflection is to identify the mistake without self-criticism. Approach this with curiosity rather than judgment. Ask yourself what happened and why it was a mistake. This inquiry clarifies the situation and sets the stage for a more thorough analysis. Next, analyze the factors that led to the mistake. Consider the specific circumstances, decisions, and actions that influenced the outcome. Were there external pressures, such as tight deadlines or conflicting priorities, or internal biases, like overconfidence or fear of failure, that shaped your choices? Understanding these elements can provide valuable insights into your decision-making process.

Another crucial aspect involves understanding the emotions tied to the mistake. Reflect on your emotional state during and after the incident. Emotions can reveal important information about your values and priorities, and recognizing them enhances your ability to navigate similar situations more effectively in the future. Accepting responsibility plays a key role in this process. While it may be tempting to blame others or external circumstances, genuine growth comes from acknowledging your role in the mistake. This doesn't mean being overly harsh on yourself; rather, it requires honesty and ownership of your actions.

Chapter 11: Digital Citizenship and Online Safety

In today's interconnected world, being a responsible digital citizen is just as important as fulfilling your obligations within your local community. Digital citizenship involves the ethical and responsible use of technology, where individuals engage in online activities with respect, integrity, and a clear understanding of their implications. It requires a thorough awareness of how actions in the digital realm can impact both oneself and others, leading to informed choices that promote a positive online environment. For a 13-year-old navigating the complexities of the digital landscape, embracing these principles is vital for creating a secure and constructive online identity.

Respecting the privacy of others is a key component of digital citizenship. This means being intentional about the information shared about yourself and those around you. Before posting a photo or sharing a personal story, take a moment to evaluate whether it respects the privacy of everyone involved. Consider whether you have received explicit permission to share the content and whether it could potentially harm or embarrass someone. Remember that once something is published online, it can be extremely difficult to remove it completely. Respecting privacy also includes recognizing the importance of protecting personal information. Avoid publicly sharing sensitive details such as your home address, phone number, or school name, as these can be exploited by malicious individuals.

Understanding your digital footprint is another critical aspect of digital citizenship. This footprint consists of the data trail created while using the internet, including social media posts, comments, search history, and online purchases. Being aware of it is essential because it can significantly shape how others view you. Colleges, employers, and even peers may examine your online presence to form opinions about your character and abilities. Therefore, it is crucial to think carefully before posting and ensure that online actions align with the image you want to project.

Recognizing credible sources is also fundamental to being a responsible digital citizen. With the vast amount of information available online, distinguishing between reliable and unreliable sources is essential. When researching a topic, prioritize information from reputable websites, such as those belonging to educational institutions, government agencies, or established news organizations. Be cautious with sites that lack author credentials or feature sensationalized headlines. Developing the ability to evaluate sources critically will empower you to make informed decisions and help prevent the spread of misinformation.

Maintaining a positive online presence goes beyond simply avoiding negative behavior; it requires actively contributing to a supportive and respectful digital community. Engaging in constructive discussions, offering encouragement, and sharing valuable content are all part of this effort. A positive online presence can lead to future opportunities, such as scholarships, internships, or job offers. Conversely, negative online behavior, such as cyberbullying or posting inappropriate content, can have lasting consequences and damage your reputation.

Social media plays a significant role in shaping your online presence. Platforms like Instagram, TikTok, and Snapchat are popular among teens, but they also come with specific responsibilities. Being mindful of the content shared and how it reflects on your character is crucial. Take the time to review your profiles. Look over posts, comments, and likes to ensure they align with the image you want to convey. If you find any content that does not reflect your values or could be misinterpreted, take action to remove it or adjust your privacy settings accordingly.

To help assess your current social media presence, consider this practical exercise: Scroll through your profiles and ask yourself the following questions: Does this content accurately represent who I am and what I stand for? Would I feel comfortable with a teacher, parent, or future employer viewing this? Are there any posts that could be misunderstood or taken out of context? This exercise can help identify areas for improvement and ensure your online presence aligns with your personal and future goals.

Real-world examples can effectively demonstrate the impact of online interactions. For instance, think about a student who used social media to raise awareness for a charitable cause, resulting in a successful fundraising campaign. This positive use of technology not only benefited the community but also enhanced the student's reputation as a proactive and compassionate individual. Conversely, there are cases where individuals have faced serious consequences for negative online behavior, such as losing job opportunities due to inappropriate posts. These examples highlight the importance of being mindful of online actions and their potential effects on your future.

Understanding online threats is essential for maintaining safety in the digital world. Phishing is a common tactic where cybercriminals trick individuals into revealing sensitive information, such as passwords or credit card numbers, by pretending to be a legitimate entity. These scams often show up as emails or messages that closely mimic the branding and communication style of reputable companies, frequently urging recipients to click on a malicious link or download a harmful attachment. To protect yourself, always check the sender's email address for any discrepancies and be cautious about unsolicited requests for personal information. If you receive a suspicious message, it's a good idea to contact the company directly using a verified phone number or their official website to confirm the legitimacy of the request.

Cyberbullying poses another significant concern, especially among adolescents. This behavior involves using digital platforms to harass, threaten, or embarrass individuals, which can occur through social media, text messages, or online forums. If you encounter cyberbullying, it's best to avoid engaging with the perpetrator. Instead, document the incidents by taking screenshots and report the behavior to the platform or a trusted adult. Many social media sites offer built-in tools for reporting inappropriate content, which can help stop bullying and protect others from similar experiences.

Identity theft is a more severe threat, where someone unlawfully acquires your personal information to commit fraud. This can happen if you share too much personal information online or fall victim to phishing scams. To safeguard your identity, be mindful of the information you share on social media and other platforms. Refrain from posting sensitive details like your full name, home address, or phone number. Regularly monitor your financial accounts for any unauthorized activity and report suspicious transactions to your bank or financial institution immediately.

Creating strong passwords is a fundamental step in securing your online accounts. A robust password should have at least 12 characters and include a mix of uppercase and lowercase letters, numbers, and special symbols. Avoid easily guessed information, such as birthdays or common words. Consider using a passphrase, which consists of a sequence of random words or a memorable sentence that is difficult for others to guess. For added security, use a unique password for each account and change them periodically, ideally every three to six months.

Two-factor authentication (2FA) adds an extra layer of security by requiring a second form of verification, such as a text message code or an authentication app, along with your password. Activating 2FA on your accounts can significantly reduce the risk of unauthorized access, even if your password is compromised.

Privacy settings on social media and other platforms are crucial for managing who can view your information and interact with you. Regularly review and update these settings to ensure they match your comfort level. For example, you can choose to make your profiles private, limit who can send you friend requests, and control who can see your posts. Being proactive about privacy settings helps protect your personal information from unauthorized access.

Antivirus software is vital for defending your devices against malware and other online threats. Keep your antivirus software up to date and run regular scans to identify and eliminate potential threats. Additionally, ensure that your operating system and applications are updated to address any security vulnerabilities that cybercriminals might exploit.

Protecting Your Privacy and Digital Reputation

In today's digital age, protecting your privacy and personal information online is super important. At 13 years old, you're probably using various social media platforms, online forums, and gaming environments. While these digital spaces are fantastic for connecting and having fun, they also require you to be mindful of the information you share. Here are some practical tips to help you safeguard your privacy and keep a positive digital reputation.

First and foremost, it's essential to be careful about the personal details you post online. Social media profiles often encourage users to share information like their full name, birthdate, school, and location. However, sharing too much personal information can put you at risk for things like identity theft, cyberbullying, or unwanted attention. To boost your safety, try to limit the personal information you reveal. For example, consider using just your first name or a nickname on your profiles. Steer clear of posting your home address, phone number, or any other sensitive details that could be misused.

Setting up strong privacy controls on your accounts is another key step in protecting your information. Most platforms offer settings that let you decide who can see your posts, send friend requests, or access your profile. Take a moment to explore these options and adjust them to match your comfort level. For instance, you might want to set your profile to private, ensuring that only approved friends can see your content. Regularly checking and updating these settings is important, as platforms often change their privacy policies and features. Staying informed and proactive helps you keep your data secure.
In online forums or gaming environments, think about using pseudonyms or avatars instead of your real name. This not only protects your identity but also adds an extra layer of privacy. When creating a username, try to avoid using any part of your real name or other identifiable information. Instead, pick something fun and unique that doesn't reveal personal details. Avatars, or digital representations of yourself, can also be a creative way to show off your personality without compromising your privacy.

Reviewing privacy policies might not sound exciting, but it's a crucial step in understanding how your data is collected and used. These documents explain what information a platform gathers, how it's stored, and who it's shared with. Getting familiar with these details helps you make informed choices about which platforms to use and what information to share. If a policy seems unclear or raises any red flags, don't hesitate to ask a trusted adult for advice.

Making it a habit to regularly check your online presence is also important. Take some time to review your social media profiles, posts, and interactions to ensure they reflect the image you want to project. If you find any content that no longer represents you or could be misunderstood, take action to remove it or adjust your privacy settings. This proactive approach helps you maintain a positive digital reputation and ensures your online presence aligns with your values and goals.
Securing personal information online is essential, and using secure communication methods is a great way to achieve this. When you send messages or emails, they travel through various networks before reaching the

intended recipient. During this journey, there's a real risk that someone unauthorized might intercept and read them. To help reduce this risk, implementing encryption is key. This complex algorithm can only be decoded by the intended recipient. By encrypting sensitive data before sharing it online, you ensure that even if someone intercepts your message, they won't be able to make sense of its contents.

Secure messaging applications and email services that offer end-to-end encryption are fantastic tools for protecting your communications. This type of encryption ensures that messages are encrypted on your device and only decrypted on the recipient's device, making it nearly impossible for anyone in between to access the content. Apps like Signal and WhatsApp are well-known for their secure messaging features, while ProtonMail is an excellent choice for encrypted email communication. To get started with these services, simply download the application or register for an account, and follow the provided instructions to enable encryption. This way, you can chat with friends and family while keeping your conversations safe from prying eyes.

Steering clear of free or public Wi-Fi networks during sensitive transactions is another important step in securing your personal information. These networks, often found in coffee shops or airports, are usually unsecured, meaning that anyone else on the same network could potentially access your data. If you need to access sensitive information, like online banking or personal accounts, using a Virtual Private Network (VPN) is a smart move. A VPN creates a secure, encrypted connection between your device and the internet, effectively shielding your data from unauthorized surveillance. To set up a VPN, choose a reputable service, download the application, and follow the setup instructions. Once connected, your online activities will be much more secure.

Being able to recognize phishing attempts is another essential skill for protecting your personal information. Phishing is a tactic used by cybercriminals to trick you into revealing sensitive information, such as passwords or credit card numbers. These scams often come in the form of emails or messages that look like they're from legitimate sources, such as your bank or a well-known website. To spot phishing attempts, keep an eye out for warning signs like generic greetings, spelling errors, or urgent requests for personal information. If you receive a suspicious email or message, avoid clicking on any links or downloading attachments. Instead, reach out to the company directly using a verified phone number or their official website to confirm whether the request is genuine.

Kind, Responsible, and Respectful Online

In the digital age, where interactions primarily occur through screens instead of face-to-face encounters, kindness takes on a more nuanced meaning. Online kindness means actively promoting empathy and understanding in every interaction, whether it's a comment on a social media post or a message in a group chat. It starts with the conscious decision to consider the emotional impact of your words before hitting "send." This involves taking a moment to think about how your message might be interpreted and whether it adds value to the discussion. Engaging in this reflective practice shows respect for others and helps create a more supportive and inclusive environment.

Positive language acts as a powerful tool in communication. The words we choose can either uplift and encourage or harm and discourage. Using supportive and constructive language can significantly brighten someone's day. For instance, if you see a friend sharing a personal achievement or showcasing a creative project, offering specific words of encouragement can boost their confidence and inspire them to pursue their interests further. Conversely, if someone faces negativity or criticism, a thoughtful and kind comment can provide essential support and reassurance.

Transforming negative interactions into positive ones through kindness is both achievable and profoundly impactful. Imagine encountering a hurtful comment on a social media post. Instead of reacting with anger or defensiveness, approach the situation with empathy. Acknowledge the other person's viewpoint and respond with understanding. For example, if someone critiques your opinion, you might say, "I understand your perspective, and I appreciate your input. Here's my reasoning for feeling differently." This approach eases tension and opens the door for constructive dialogue and mutual respect.

Practicing gratitude online serves as another effective strategy for spreading kindness. Recognizing the contributions of others—whether it's a helpful comment, a shared resource, or a creative idea—enhances a sense of community and appreciation. Simple gestures, such as thanking someone for their insights or expressing gratitude for a shared experience, strengthen connections and foster a positive atmosphere. For instance, if a classmate provides study tips that significantly aid your exam preparation, sending a brief message of thanks effectively conveys your appreciation and encourages them to continue sharing their expertise.

Real-world examples highlight the impact of kindness in digital interactions. Picture a scenario where a student receives critical feedback on a project shared online. Instead of feeling disheartened, they receive supportive comments from peers who offer constructive suggestions and words of encouragement. This positive reinforcement not only helps the student improve their work but also boosts their confidence and motivation. In another instance, a group of friends might use a chat to exchange daily affirmations or positive quotes, creating an environment where everyone feels valued and supported.

Incorporating kindness into online interactions goes beyond mere niceness; it involves actively building a digital community where everyone feels respected and valued. Promoting empathy, using positive language, and practicing gratitude contribute to a culture of kindness that can have a lasting impact on both online and offline relationships. Remember that your words carry weight, and choosing kindness can significantly influence the interactions you have.

In the realm of digital interactions, taking responsibility is crucial. A significant aspect of this involves verifying the accuracy of the information shared. Before posting or forwarding any content, it's essential to check its authenticity. This means examining the source, seeking corroborating evidence from reputable outlets, and being cautious of sensationalized headlines that lack credible backing. Implementing these verification steps helps prevent the spread of misinformation, which can lead to misunderstandings and potentially harmful consequences.

Acknowledging mistakes is vital for accountability in online actions. If you realize that you've shared incorrect information or made a hurtful comment, issuing a sincere apology is important. This shows maturity and a willingness to learn from errors. An effective apology should be direct, recognize the specific mistake, and express a commitment to improve future behavior. For instance, if you posted something that turned out to be false, you might say, "I apologize for sharing incorrect information earlier. I've since verified the facts and will exercise greater caution in the future."

Managing time spent on social media is another important aspect of being a responsible digital citizen. It's easy to lose track of time while scrolling through feeds or watching videos, which can lead to neglecting other important responsibilities like homework, chores, or spending quality time with family. To maintain a healthy balance, consider setting specific time limits for social media use. You can use apps that track and limit screen time or establish personal goals to gradually reduce usage. Allocating designated times of the day for social media, such as after completing homework or during scheduled breaks, can help ensure it doesn't interfere with other obligations.

Recognizing and handling cyberbullying is a critical skill for maintaining a respectful online environment. It can take many forms, including hurtful comments, spreading rumors, or sharing embarrassing content. If you encounter cyberbullying, whether as a target or a bystander, it's important to take action. Document the incidents by taking screenshots and report the behavior to the platform or a trusted adult. Many social media sites have built-in tools for reporting inappropriate content, which can help stop the bullying and protect others from similar experiences.

If you find yourself being bullied online, remember that you are not alone and that support is available. Reach out to friends, family, or school counselors who can provide guidance and assistance. It's also important to avoid engaging with the bully, as this can escalate the situation. Instead, focus on building a supportive network and participating in positive online interactions.

For those witnessing cyberbullying, offering support to the victim can make a significant difference. A simple message of encouragement or standing up against the bully in a respectful manner can help the victim feel less isolated. Encouraging them to report the behavior and seek help is also crucial.

Respecting diverse opinions and backgrounds serves as a cornerstone for maintaining respect in online communication. In a digital environment where individuals from various cultures and experiences come together, approaching interactions with an open mind and a commitment to understanding different perspectives is essential. This means actively listening to others, even when their views differ from your own. Active listening involves focusing on the speaker's words, asking specific clarifying questions to ensure comprehension, and thoughtfully reflecting on their points before formulating a response. This practice not only demonstrates respect but also enhances your understanding of the subject matter.

When participating in online discussions, responding constructively is crucial. Such responses add value to the conversation by providing insights or posing questions that advance the dialogue. For example, if someone shares an opinion you disagree with, instead of dismissing it outright, you might say, "I understand your viewpoint, and I appreciate your perspective. Here's my interpretation..." This approach fosters a respectful exchange of ideas and can lead to more meaningful conversations.

Avoiding arguments is another key aspect of respectful online communication. While encountering differing opinions is common, engaging in heated disputes rarely leads to productive outcomes. Instead, focus on identifying common ground or agreeing to disagree when necessary. If a discussion becomes overly contentious, it may be wise to step back and evaluate whether continuing the conversation is beneficial. It's perfectly okay to disengage from a discussion that isn't yielding constructive results.

Being a responsible digital citizen means more than just following rules—it's about choosing kindness, verifying information, and respecting others online. Your words and actions can shape the digital world, so always strive to support, uplift, and protect yourself and others. Remember, every positive interaction helps build a safer, more inclusive online community.

Chapter 12: Financial Literacy for Beginners

Financial literacy is a vital skill set that empowers you to achieve personal independence and long-term success. At its core, it includes the knowledge and skills necessary for making informed and effective decisions about financial resources. This encompasses essential concepts such as income, expenses, savings, and budgeting. Let's dive into these components to understand how they can positively impact your life.

Income refers to the total amount of money you receive, which can come from various sources like a part-time job, allowances, gifts, or freelance work. This figure serves as the foundation for your financial planning. Expenses, on the other hand, represent the costs you incur, including everyday purchases like snacks, clothing, or entertainment. Effectively managing these two components is crucial for maintaining stability.

Savings is the portion of your income that you intentionally set aside for future needs or goals. This practice is akin to investing in your future well-being. Whether you're saving for a new electronic device, a special occasion, or higher education, having a savings plan allows you to make choices without the weight of financial anxiety. A budget is a structured plan that helps you manage income and expenses. It serves as a strategic framework, guiding you on how to allocate resources to meet your needs and achieve your objectives.

Acquiring money management skills from an early age proves invaluable. These skills equip you to make informed decisions that can significantly influence your daily life and future opportunities. For example, knowing how to create a budget can help you decide whether to spend your allowance on a new video game or save it for a more significant purchase. This knowledge also helps you distinguish between needs—such as food and shelter—and wants, which are non-essential items like the latest gaming console.

Let's explore the fundamentals of budgeting. Start by carefully tracking your income and expenses. This involves keeping a detailed record of all financial inflows and outflows. You can use a notebook, a digital spreadsheet, or a budgeting application for this purpose. Once you have a comprehensive overview of your financial landscape, formulate a straightforward weekly budget. Document your income sources and project your expenses. Designate a specific percentage of your income for savings, ensuring that total expenses do not exceed income.

To apply this practically, create a weekly budget. Begin by itemizing your expected income for the week. Next, outline your anticipated expenses, categorizing them into needs and wants. Allocate a defined amount for savings, even if it is a modest sum. This exercise will enhance your understanding of spending patterns and enable you to adjust your financial behavior to align with your goals.

Establishing financial goals is another essential element of financial literacy. These goals can range from short-term objectives, such as saving for a concert ticket, to long-term aspirations, like funding a college education. Clearly defined goals provide direction and motivation for your savings efforts. They also help you prioritize expenditures, ensuring that financial resources are utilized effectively.

Consider a practical example: Suppose you aim to purchase a new bicycle. Setting a specific financial goal allows you to calculate the amount you need to save each week to reach your target. This may require you to reduce discretionary spending, such as cutting back on snacks or seeking additional income opportunities. Progressing toward your goal will cultivate discipline and a sense of achievement, both of which are essential skills for future financial success.

Managing your money requires a clear understanding of the specific features and functions of various types of bank accounts. Two common types are savings and checking accounts. A savings account helps you accumulate funds over time and typically offers interest, meaning the bank pays you a small percentage of your balance as an incentive for keeping your money there. This interest can lead to gradual growth of your savings, making it a great way to watch your money grow. In contrast, a checking account is designed for frequent transactions, such as buying lunch or paying for a movie ticket. It usually comes with a debit card, allowing easy access to your funds for everyday expenses.

Opening a bank account is a straightforward process that requires specific documentation. You will need to visit a bank with a parent or guardian, as minors often need an adult to co-sign the account. Bring identification, such as a birth certificate or school ID, along with proof of address, like a utility bill or lease agreement. A bank representative will guide you through the necessary paperwork and explain the account's features, including any fees or minimum balance requirements. Maintaining a positive relationship with your bank is important because it can lead to benefits such as reduced fees, better interest rates, and access to personalized financial advice.

Interest is a key concept in financial literacy. When you deposit money into a savings account, the bank uses those funds to lend to other customers. In return, they pay you interest, calculated as a percentage of your balance. Over time, this can significantly enhance your savings. For example, if you deposit $100 in a savings account with a 2% annual interest rate, you will earn $2 in interest after one year, resulting in a total of $102. While this may seem minimal at first, the interest can accumulate over several years, especially if you continue to make additional deposits.

Money Basics and Smart Budgeting

Try using the 50/30/20 rule to manage your allowance: 50% for needs, 30% for wants, and 20% for savings. This simple method helps you cover essentials, enjoy fun purchases, and build your savings—all at the same time. Start tracking your spending with a notebook or budgeting app, and review your expenses weekly. Small, consistent steps now can lead to big financial confidence later!

Managing your allowance or earnings is a key step toward achieving financial independence and honing your money management skills. One of the first things you can do is set aside a specific percentage of your income for savings as soon as you receive it. This habit not only helps you build a financial cushion for those unexpected expenses but also encourages discipline and strategic planning. Think of savings as a proactive way to ensure you have funds ready for emergencies or to reach your financial goals.

To manage your finances effectively, break down your income into three clear categories: savings, spending, and giving. This organized approach allows you to distribute your resources in a way that meets your essential needs, allows for some fun spending, and supports charitable contributions or helping others. A popular budgeting method is the '50/30/20 rule,' which suggests allocating 50% of your income to needs, 30% to wants, and 20% to savings. This guideline offers a simple way to handle your financial responsibilities without feeling overwhelmed.

Let's put the 50/30/20 rule into action with your allowance. If you receive $50 each month, set aside $25 (50%) for essential needs, like school supplies or transportation costs. Then, allocate $15 (30%) for discretionary wants, such as a new video game or a movie night. Finally, reserve $10 (20%) for savings aimed at future goals or emergency funds. This strategy ensures you cover necessary expenses while still enjoying a portion of your earnings and boosting your savings.

Setting savings goals is another important aspect of financial literacy. These goals can range from short-term objectives, like saving for a new pair of sneakers, to long-term dreams, such as building a fund for college tuition. Having clear objectives helps keep you motivated and focused on your financial targets. To create effective savings goals, start by identifying what you want to achieve and estimating the total cost. Then, figure out how much you need to save each week or month to reach your target within a specific timeframe.

For example, if you want to buy a bicycle that costs $200 within six months, you would need to save about $33 per month. This might mean adjusting your spending habits, like cutting back on snacks or finding ways to earn a little extra income. Setting realistic and achievable goals allows you to track your progress and celebrate your successes along the way.

Here's a "Try This" activity to help you create a savings plan for a specific goal. First, choose an item or experience you want to save for, like a concert ticket or a new gadget. Next, find out the total cost and set a deadline for when you want to achieve this goal. Calculate how much you need to save each week or month to hit your target. Finally, make a visual savings tracker, like a chart or a jar, to keep an eye on your progress and stay motivated. This exercise will help you develop a practical savings plan while reinforcing the importance of financial discipline and goal-setting.

Understanding expenses plays a crucial role in effective financial management. It's essential to track your spending carefully. You can do this by keeping a detailed expense log, which acts as a comprehensive record of all your financial transactions. Whether you opt for a physical notebook, a digital spreadsheet, or a specialized budgeting app, documenting each purchase will help you analyze trends in your spending behavior and pinpoint specific categories where you might be overspending.

For a 13-year-old, typical expenses might include snacks, social outings with friends, or hobbies like buying art supplies or video games. Systematic recording allows for a clear understanding of spending in each category. This awareness is the foundational step toward making informed financial decisions.

Budgeting apps can be especially helpful for monitoring expenses. Many of these applications offer features that let you categorize spending, set limits, and receive notifications when you're nearing your budget threshold for a specific category. If you prefer a more hands-on approach, a simple notebook can work just as well. The key is consistency—make it a habit to record every expense, no matter how small.

Regularly analyzing your spending habits is important. Set aside time each week to review your expense log. Look for patterns or areas where you could cut back. For example, if you notice that snack purchases are unusually high, consider preparing snacks at home instead of buying them. Adjusting your budget based on these insights can help you save money and reach your financial goals more quickly.

Real-life scenarios highlight the importance of making financial trade-offs. Imagine you have $20 to spend for the week. You want to buy a new book and go to a movie with friends, but doing both would exceed your budget. In this situation, you need to make a choice. You could borrow the book from the library and use the money for the movie, or you might decide to skip the movie and invest in the book. These decisions help prioritize spending based on your values and interests.

Here's a practical exercise to help you categorize your recent expenses into needs and wants. Start by listing all expenses from the past week. Next to each item, mark whether it is a need or a want. Needs include essential items like school supplies or transportation, while wants are non-essential items such as a new video game or a specialty coffee. This exercise will clarify areas where you might reduce spending and increase savings.

A thorough understanding and effective tracking of expenses enable you to make more informed financial decisions. This process not only helps manage your current finances but also sets the stage for more advanced financial planning in the future. As you refine these skills, you'll find that managing money becomes increasingly straightforward and instinctive.

Unexpected expenses can pop up when you least expect them, so being ready for these surprises is a vital part of financial literacy. Establishing an emergency fund is a smart strategy to tackle this. This fund is a special savings account set aside for those unforeseen costs, like an unexpected school trip costing $200 or a $150 repair for a broken smartphone. It's important to build this fund gradually. Start by regularly setting aside a specific percentage of your income, even if it's just $5 each week. Over time, these consistent contributions can grow into a significant financial cushion, providing both peace of mind and improved security.

When income decreases or unexpected costs arise, prioritizing expenses becomes essential. Identify your most critical needs first, such as purchasing essential school supplies or covering transportation costs. Make sure to address these needs before anything else. You can temporarily reduce or eliminate non-essential items, like entertainment subscriptions or dining out, to redirect funds toward more pressing requirements. This approach helps maintain stability and ensures that essential needs are consistently met.

Finding creative ways to save money can lead to significant benefits. Engaging in DIY projects not only reduces expenses but also brings a sense of achievement. For example, creating your own gifts or home decorations can be both enjoyable and cost-effective. Explore free activities in your community, such as local festivals, library workshops, or nature hikes. These options offer entertainment and personal growth without straining your finances.

Discussing financial decisions with family members or trusted adults can provide valuable insights and guidance. They can share their experiences and offer practical advice on effective money management. This conversation can help you understand different perspectives and strategies for navigating challenges. Don't hesitate to ask questions or seek advice when you're uncertain about a decision. Learning from others can significantly enhance your financial literacy and decision-making skills.

Smart Choices: Saving, Spending, and Financial Goals

Making informed decisions about money is a vital skill that can greatly shape your financial future. This process involves carefully analyzing options and considering the long-term effects of your financial choices. It's not just about deciding whether to buy something now or wait; it's about understanding how each decision fits into your overall financial strategy and goals.

A key step in making sound financial decisions is distinguishing between wants and needs. Needs are essential items or services critical for survival and well-being, such as nutritious food, appropriate clothing, and safe housing. In contrast, wants are discretionary items that enhance lifestyle but aren't vital, like the latest gaming console or trendy shoes. Recognizing this distinction is crucial for prioritizing your spending and ensuring that your basic needs are met before indulging in non-essential desires.

When faced with a purchasing decision, it's important to assess the value and necessity of the item in question. Ask yourself some key questions: "Is this item essential for my current situation?" "Will this enhance my quality of life in a meaningful way?" "Are there more cost-effective alternatives available?" Reflecting on these questions can help curb impulse purchases and lead to more thoughtful choices that align with your financial goals.

Creating a prioritized list is an effective strategy for managing your expenditures. Start by listing all the items you wish to purchase or save for, then rank them based on their importance. This list will guide your spending decisions, helping you figure out which purchases should be made right away and which can wait. For example, if your budget is tight, you might prioritize saving for a new laptop that's essential for your studies over buying a new video game.

Try this activity to practice financial prioritization: Write down your top five financial priorities and explain why each one matters to you. Reflect on the significance of each item and how it aligns with your long-term financial aspirations. This exercise will deepen your understanding of your financial values and empower you to make more informed spending choices.

Aligning your spending habits with your personal values and goals is another important aspect of financial literacy. Values are the guiding principles that shape your decisions and actions, while goals are the specific financial outcomes you aim to achieve. Ensuring that your expenditures reflect your values and support your goals allows for more meaningful and fulfilling financial decisions.

Smart spending choices help you reach larger financial objectives by enabling better resource allocation. For instance, if your goal is to save for college tuition, making intentional decisions to cut back on discretionary spending can speed up your progress toward that goal. Similarly, if you prioritize environmental sustainability, you might choose to invest in eco-friendly products, even if they come with a higher initial cost, because they resonate with your values and contribute to a healthier planet.

Understanding the implications of your financial decisions and aligning them with your values and goals fosters a more strategic approach to managing your finances. This not only helps you achieve immediate financial targets but also sets the stage for long-term financial success. As you continue to sharpen your money management skills, making informed decisions will become second nature, empowering you to tackle life's financial challenges with confidence and competence.

Setting realistic and achievable financial goals is essential for managing your money effectively. These goals can be divided into two categories: short-term and long-term. Short-term goals are those you aim to achieve within a year, like saving $300 for a new smartphone or $200 for a special occasion, such as a birthday party. On the other hand, long-term goals might involve saving $20,000 for college tuition or $15,000 for a car purchase, which require more time and thoughtful planning. Both types are important because they provide direction and motivation, helping you focus your efforts and allocate resources wisely.
Breaking large goals into smaller, manageable steps is key to success. This approach transforms overwhelming tasks into achievable actions and allows you to track your progress more effectively. For instance, if your goal is to save $500 for a new laptop within a year, you can break it down to saving about $42 each month. This smaller target feels less intimidating and offers a clear, actionable path to follow. Setting specific milestones, like saving $125 every three months, can also create a sense of accomplishment and keep you motivated.

Staying motivated is crucial for reaching your financial goals. One effective strategy is to visualize the end result and remind yourself of the tangible benefits it will bring, such as increased productivity or enhanced learning opportunities. Creating a vision board or placing a picture of your goal in a visible spot can serve as a constant reminder of what you're working towards. Another helpful tip is to reward yourself for reaching milestones. These rewards don't have to be extravagant; simple treats, like enjoying a favorite meal or having a movie night, can be just as satisfying. Celebrating small victories can lift your spirits and encourage you to keep pushing forward.

Tracking your progress is another important aspect of goal-setting. Regularly reviewing your savings and spending habits helps you stay on track and make necessary adjustments. You can use a spreadsheet, a budgeting app, or even a simple notebook to document your progress. Keeping a close eye on your financial activities allows you to pinpoint specific areas where you might need to cut back, such as dining out or subscription services, or discover ways to boost savings, like taking on a side job or selling unused items.

www.ingramcontent.com/pod-product-compliance
Lightning Source LLC
Chambersburg PA
CBHW060350190426
43201CB00043B/1912